Coming to some Conclusions on Leadership Style

(A Paper for use in ML 500/520 Introduction to Leadership)

by

Dr. J. Robert Clinton
Associate Professor of Leadership
School of World Mission
Fuller Theological Seminary

ISBN 1-932814-19-1

copyright © 1992 J. Robert Clinton

Table of Contents

Page	Item
7	INTRODUCTION
9	I. WHY STUDY LEADERSHIP STYLES?
11	II. WHERE IT FITS IN LEADERSHIP THEORY
11	A. Background
12	B. A Simple Tracing of the Paradigmatic Eras
13	Figure 1. Paradigm Shift from Pre-Modern to Modern Era
14	Figure 2. Major Paradigm Shift—Leadership Research
14	Figure 3. Trait Theory Era Identified
15	Figure 4. Major Research Foci—First Three Eras
16	Figure 5. Simplified Paradigmatic Time-Line
19	Table 1. Full Time-Line of Leadership History
20	Figure 6. Tree Diagram—Leadership Categories
23	III. SOME VARIOUS POSITIONS
23	A. Introduction
23	B. Some observations from Downey
25	Table 2. Some Leadership Taxonomies
28	Figure 7. Hill's Four Leadership Styles
29	C. Three Differing Views
29	1. Background
30	Figure 8. Style Approaches—Contingency Models
31	Table 3. Comparison of Style Theorists
32	2. One Ideal Style—Mouton-Blake Approach

4		Coming to Some Conclusions on Leadership Styles
33		3. One Fixed Style—Fiedler
34		4. Multi-style Approach—Hersey and Blanchard's Approach
35		5. Summary of the Three Approaches
36		6. Shawchuck's Emphasis
37		7. Where to Now?
39	IV.	TOWARD DEFINITIONS
39		A. Introduction
39		B. Situational Leadership Style Defined
40		C. Leadership Style Bent Defined
41		D. Dominant Leadership Style Defined
41		1. Directive—Non-Directive Continuum
42		Figure 9. Hersey and Blanchard Categories Equated To Directive Categories
43		2. Relating Hersey and Blanchard to Biblical Styles
43		Figure 10. Biblical Styles Equated to Hersey and Blanchard and Directive Scales
43		E. 4 Major Factors Which Influence Leadership Style
43		1. Functional Notation of Factors
44		2. Leader Personality Bent (L_{per})
46		Figure 11. Relationship Between Major Personality Factors
47		Figure 12. Inflexibility—Flexibility Continuum
47		3. Leader Function (L_{fn})
49		4. Follower Maturity (F_{mat})
50		5. Leader-Follower Relationship ($L\text{-}F_{rel}$)
51		Figure 13. Leader-Follower Relationship Continuum
51		6. Summary of Leadership Factors Affecting Style
55	V.	STEPS IN STYLE ANALYSIS
55		Table 4. 7 Steps in Style Analysis

Table of Contents   5

59	VI.	**OBSERVATIONS ON PAULINE LEADERSHIP STYLES**
59		A. 10 Styles Observed
59		1. Apostolic—highly directive
60		2. Confrontation—highly directive
61		3. Father-Initiator—highly directive
62		4. Obligation-Persuasion—directive
63		5. Father-Guardian—directive
63		6. Maturity Appeal—directive/non-directive
64		7. Nurse—non-directive
65		8. Imitator—non-directive/highly non-directive
66		9. Consensus—highly non-directive
67		10. Indirect Conflict—highly non-directive
67		B. Doohan's Observations on Pauline Leadership
70		C. Summary of Lessons
73	VII.	**MISCELLANEOUS CONCEPTS RELATING TO LEADERSHIP STYLE**
73		A. Introduction
73		B. The Organizational Coherence Continuum
74		Figure 14. The Organizational Coherence Continuum
75		C. Power Concepts of Wrong and Mintzberg
76		Figure 15. Wrong and Mintzberg and the Continuum
76		D. Some Final Suggestions on Power and Leadership Style
79		**SUMMARY AND CONCLUSION**
85		Appendix A. Contingency Theory Concepts
99		Appendix B. Supplementary Bibliography on Leadership Styles
105		Appendix C. Some Power Concepts of Wrong and Mintzberg
111		Bibliography

Coming to Some Conclusions on Leadership Styles

Introduction

Leaders influence.[1] It's that simple. But how do they influence? It's not so simple. Leadership style deals with that not-so-simple subject—how a leader individually and collectively influences followers. The term leadership style is bandied about quite regularly. Yet few leaders can define it. Few leaders can analyze it. Few leaders can apply any thinking about it in such a way as to alter their means of influence. This article takes initial steps to correct these neglects. It is the purpose of this article to clarify some issues concerning leadership style. It will point out the complexity of the subject. It will show my own opinions to date. While not complete, the paper is a good start on the subject. Perhaps it will be enough of a jumping-off point to stimulate other Christian leaders to research this subject in the context of Christian leadership.

It is the thesis of this paper that the study of leadership style

1) first, requires historical analysis of the concept,

2) needs to be correlated with leadership theory as a whole,

3) became the focus of leadership theory during the Ohio State Era and the Contingency Era of leadership history,

4) points out the complexity involved in leadership influence,

5) is foundational to the training and development of leaders,

---

[1] The definition we are presently using in the leadership concentration highlights this essential function.

A *leader* in the Biblical context for which we are interested in studying selection and training is a person with God-given capacity and with God-given responsibility to INFLUENCE a specific group of God's people toward God's purposes for the group. (Clinton, 1984:11)

It is this function—influence, not role—which is at the heart of all leadership.

6) requires reflection from a Christian standpoint (most leadership style theory has come from secular leadership theorists),

7) is in need of further research from a missiological standpoint.

The structure of the paper attempts to develop or suggest the above ideas. Section I suggest three reasons for studying leadership style. While many reasons could be given, these highlight personal growth and responsibility. Section II deals with points 1, 2, and 3 which all concern the historical background in which leadership style theory arose. Concepts are always best understood when seen in light of the times that prompted them. Sections III, IV, and V deal either directly or indirectly with points 4 and 5. Section VI discusses leadership styles in terms of scriptural observations. Section VII and the conclusion talk about point 7.

I.
Why Study Leadership Styles?

Why should a Christian leader study leadership styles? Let me at this point suggest three basic reasons without offering proof of them. Even without proof they will probably shift the question from "why study leadership styles" to "why not study leadership styles?"

In my travels and consultations concerning leadership issues I have noticed much conflict between leaders and followers. Some is necessary and comes as a result of conviction concerning Christianity. But much of it does not deal with Christian convictions. Conflict in ministry often hinges around the leadership style of the leader. Failure to recognize leadership style as a key issue in ministry conflict aggravates the situation.[2] Identification of factors concerning leadership style allows for adjustments which may lessen ministry conflict. Apparently, different leadership situations demand different styles. Ignorance of styles lessens the chances that a leader can adjust style to meet situation. So Reason Number One is a simple one. *A leader who wants to avoid unnecessary conflict needs to know about leadership styles.*

Leaders should be concerned about training followers.[3] Leaders who are trained in leadership style theory not only are better leaders, but they also are more conscious of developing leaders and followers under them. Leaders who study leadership styles have an increased sensitivity toward

---

[2] See Norman Shawchuck's article, "Are You A Flexible Leader?" in **Leadership,** Spring 1983. His opening attention-getter is a mini-case study which describes a pastor in his third pastorate. The thrust of the mini-case study is just this very fact. The pastor failed to see that his leadership style was the primary cause of the conflict in the church which eventually led to his resignation.

[3] This it the thrust of the Ephesians 4:7–16 passage. Christian leadership at all levels should have leadership selection and training as a major function. And it should be high in priority. Leadership transition is a major organizational problem in Christian institutions because leadership selection and training is not considered as a major upper level leadership function.

followers and recognize that leadership style will directly affect followers' rate of development. Reason Number Two, then, suggests that *leaders aware of a variety of styles will use styles most appropriate to the developing of followers.* They will be concerned not only with being effective leaders but developing effective leaders.

Leaders are responsible before God for developing their capacity as leaders. We know from the central truths of the stewardship parables[4] that as leaders we will be accountable to God for developing and using our capacities. Most leaders have greater capacity for varying leadership styles than they presently do. The study of leadership styles is a step toward developing your capacity as a leader. Reason Number Three then suggests that *a leader should study leadership styles in order to expand capacity to lead.*

---

[4] By stewardship parables I mean those parables which point out that leaders will give an account for Kingdom ministry. Two important parables include the "Parable of the Pounds" in Luke 19 and the "Parable of the Talents" in Matthew 25.

II.
Where it Fits in Leadership Theory

A. Background

I have found it helpful in my own understanding of leadership styles to see how and why the emphasis of studying leadership styles came about. This requires a quick look at the history of leadership theory.

In my paper,[5] "A Paradigmatic Overview of the Leadership Field From 1841-1986," I show that historically, from a paradigmatic viewpoint, modern leadership research and theory can be viewed in 5 phases:

>   Phase I.   Great Man Era: 1841-1904
>   Phase II. Trait Era: 1904-1948
>   Phase III. Behavior Era: 1948-1967
>   Phase IV. Contingency Era: 1967-1980
>   Phase V.   Complexity Era: 1980-1986

Two items of that statement need further explaining—modern leadership research and theory, and paradigmatic viewpoint.

The scientific thinking process being introduced in the early nineteenth century began to impact people writing about leadership from the mid 1800s on. I call this the modern leadership research era. It is characterized by at least two major influences. One, the scientific method of observation, deduction, and replication of findings prevailed as the more sophisticated approach to obtain truth. Two, modern communication networks began to build so that written information could be transmitted more readily. This meant that researchers could learn of other findings

---

[5] This paper, "A Paradigmatic Overview of the Leadership Field from 1841-1986," is available from Barnabas Resources, 2175 N. Holliston Avenue, Altadena, CA 91001.

and build upon them. There was the possibility of connected threads of zin an area of study, hence the possibility of dominant paradigms.

I am using paradigm to mean a dominant research approach which was followed by the majority of researchers during a given specified time period. I am using it somewhat analogously to Kuhn (1970). The identification of a dominant research approach and the tracing of it over a period of time until it no longer dominates underlies the five-fold outline given above. Usually a dominating research approach is replaced by another newer approach which seems better to answer the anomalies of a previous approach. When such a new paradigm comes in, we describe this as a paradigm shift.[6] Sometimes remnants of the old remain. At other times the old is discarded. The study of leadership paradigms and paradigm shifts gives a broad contextual framework upon which a leadership student can build. Present day research, including the study of leadership styles, is better understood in the light of this historic paradigmatic viewpoint.

In order to see where leadership styles fits into the history of leadership theory it is helpful if we view leadership theory in terms of the major paradigms. I do this along a time-line. Let me give the sequence of analysis that leads me to Figure 5 which gives a simplified time-line which contains 5 phases. Then I will give Table 1 which is a more complicated summary of this historical time-line.

B. A Simple Tracing of the Paradigmatic Eras

In terms of paradigmatic eras two major breaks occur. The first major break was somewhere in the mid 1800s. The second major break occurred in 1948. Figure 1 depicts the first major break. Figure 2 shows the second major break.

Several differences characterize the eras on either side of this first major break. I have listed three which are significant to the history of leadership theory as viewed paradigmatically.

---

[6] See Kuhn (1970) for development of paradigmatic theory. See Kraft (1977), Chapter 2, "Mirrors of Reality", for application of the paradigm shift concept to ethno-theological concerns.

Where it Fits in Leadership Theory

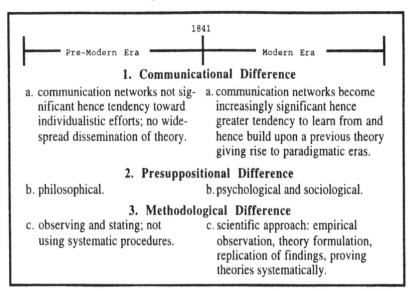

Figure 1. Paradigm Shift from Pre-Modern Era to Modern Era

The second major break occurred in 1948. The Trait Theory which had dominated the research approach for some forty years was proving to be a fruitless endeavor.[7] A series of reviews of what had been accomplished during the Trait Era occurred in the mid-forties. Stogdill's paper concluded this critical trend of the trait era. It brought about the major paradigm shift in the study of leadership. Leadership theory took a major turn, its most major shift, at that point.

---

[7] Trait Theory is broken up into two categories. Early Trait Theory had as its focus the differentiation of traits between leaders and followers. It was the dominating research paradigm from 1904 to 1948. Latter Trait Theory had as its focus the identification of traits of leaders demonstrating successful behavior in various industrial leadership roles. It has not been a dominant paradigm, but has persisted from the fifties to the present.

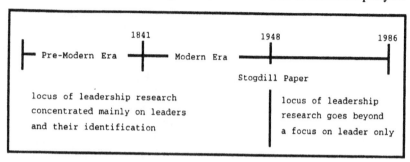

Figure 2. Major Paradigm Shift in Locus of Leadership Research

Stogdill's paper was originally entitled "Personal Factors Associated With Leadership: A Survey of the Literature" and was printed in the **Journal of Psychology,** 1948, 25, 35-71. When Bass (1981) revised Stogdill's magnum opus (1974) he included Stogdill's paper intact in Chapter 4 which he entitled "Leadership Traits: 1904-1947." Bass' reckoning helps us pinpoint the length of the trait era. Our time-line becomes in terms of paradigms as seen in Figure 3.

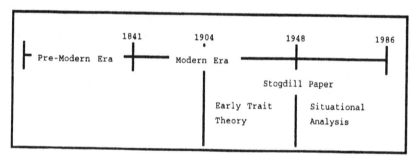

Figure 3. Trait Theory Era Identified

Prior to the turn of the century theorists such as Carlyle, Galton, Woods and James concentrated on the study of "Great Men." That is, they studied people who had significantly affected history. This focus is significantly different from the trait paradigm which followed.

Figure 4 illustrates this along the time-line.

Where it Fits in Leadership Theory

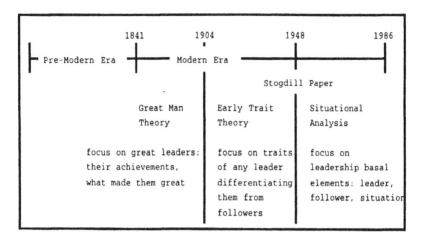

Figure 4. Major Research Foci: Great Man, Early Trait Era, Post-Stogdill

In line with Toffler's (1970) general observations[8] and Whitehead's acute paradigmatic insight,[9] the pace of change increased much more

---

[8] Toffler's **Future Shock** stresses the importance of recognizing the pace of change.

[9] Alfred North Whitehead's observation, given at a commencement address at Harvard University in 1930, is worthy of note in this regard.

> Throughout history, until the first quarter of the twentieth century, the life-span of an individual was less than the time-span of major cultural change. Under this condition it was appropriate to define education as a process of transmittal of what is known—of transmitting the culture. It was also appropriate to define the role of the teacher as that of transmitter of information and to regard education as an agency for youth.... We are living in the first period of human history for which this is assumption is false.... Today this time span is considerably shorter than that of human life, and accordingly our training must prepare individuals to face a novelty of conditions. [Knowles adds further,]... in other words, as the time-span of major cultural change has become shorter than the life-span of the individual, it becomes necessary to redefine education as a process of continuing inquiry. The role of teacher must shift from that of transmitter of information to facilitator and resource to self-directed inquiry, and to regard education as a lifelong process. For knowledge gained at any point of time will become increasingly obsolete in the course of time. (Knowles 1980:40,41)

The implications of this observation are slowly penetrating educational circles. The implications for training in this rapid pace of change as seen by Whitehead has had rapidly. Great Man theory lasted about 60 plus years. Early Trait Theory prevailed for about 40 years. The next paradigm, the Ohio State research emphasis and its spin-offs, lasted for about 20 years. Fleishman's paper (1973)[10] described the thinking that led to that paradigm. Fiedler's Contingency Model (1967) and spin-offs or alternate situational models have dominated for almost 15 years. And presently we are in an era of complex models.

It is the Contingency Era in general, and Fiedler in particular, that brought focus on the study of leadership styles. I will come back to this point after giving Figure 5—the simplified overview of leadership history viewed paradigmatically. Figure 5 shows the complete time-line in simplified form.

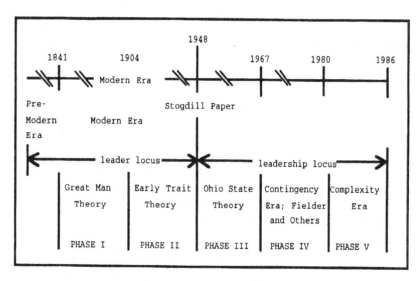

Figure 5. Simplified Paradigmatic Time-Line of Leadership Theory

---

very little, if any, impact on theological education. This notion needs to be acknowledged and should dominate curriculum design in theological education.

[10] Fleishman's (1973) paper, "Twenty Years of Consideration and Structure," reveals the feelings of one who as a doctoral student experienced this paradigm shift. He describes the actual shifts, the prevailing view, the research that sparked the new paradigm and the outworking of the new paradigm.

The reactionary trend toward authoritarian leadership in the decade of the 1950's[11] led toward a more democratic trend in leadership. McGregor[12] and others pushed the trend in industry. Blake and Mouton built upon the findings of the Ohio State Era, which focused in general on two major leadership behaviors called "consideration" and "initiation of structure,"[13] and in light of the trend toward a more democratic trend opted for their "Managerial Grid" which stressed equal balance upon a concern for production and a concern for people. While not identifying their approach as a leadership style approach, in essence it was a major step toward leadership style thinking. The difference was that concern for production and concern for people was seen in Blake and Mouton's work as part of a value system managers should have and not tied to their personality.

Fiedler went further and tied leadership style to personality. I identify the termination date of the behavior phase (the Ohio State Era) with Fiedler's publication of **A Theory of Leadership Effectiveness**. In it Fiedler explains in detail his contingency model of leadership. Bass notes that "Fiedler's (1967) contingency model of leadership is the most widely researched on leadership. At the same time, it is the most widely criticized (Bass 1981:341). It was this theory which radically shifted the focus of leadership study from behavioral analysis in general to leadership style analysis in particular. It also expanded the variables of leadership being studied beyond just a focus on leadership behavior to include followers and situation. This thematic focus highlighted leadership

---

[11] This is an instance of macro-context elements impacting on the entire leadership field. Adorno et al (1950) had done their famous research on authoritarian personalities (Hitler, Mussolini, etc.) as a reaction to World War II (Holocaust). There was a mega-trend against authoritarian leadership. The pendulum often swings more than necessary in order to correct an imbalance.

[12] McGregor and others carried this contextual macro-trend directly into the leadership field. They reacted against authoritarian leadership and toward democratic/participative styles of management. This ramified to theological education as well. See Wagner's **Leading Your Church to Grow**. Wagner recognized this trend and describes seminary thrusts in the sixties as having produced facilitator-type leadership rather than strong leadership. He is writing in the throes of the countertrend to authoritarian leadership and thus advocates strong leadership to bring about church growth.

[13] Consideration refers to leadership behavior which is relationship oriented. Initiation of structure refers to leadership behavior which is task oriented.

variables, a trend typical of the fifth development phase—the Complexity Era.

I summarize the paradigmatic view of the history of leadership theory in a Table form which compares several items.

Where it Fits in Leadership Theory

	I → Great Man 1841	II → Trait 1904	← III → Behavior 1948	← IV → Contingency 1967	← V → Complexity 1980 1986
boundary conditions		Psychological Sociological entry into leadership	Stodgill's research paper	Fielder's book	plethora of publications dealing with complexity of leadership elements
methodology	biographical	sociometry empirical exper. field exper. statistics	increasingly behavioral science methodology questionnaires e.g. LBDQ factor analysis	same as III more toward micro/ empirical questionnaires e.g. LPC	same as III trend toward macro/
focus on	leader	leader attributes	leader behavior	leadership styles; situational elements of leadership	organizational culture & other larger macro elements of leadership
end result	principles rule of thumb	lists of qualities	measurements of behavior functions such as initiation, consideration	measurements of style correlated to other elements	? my guess toward two extremes: pragmatic; philosophical applications
dominant theory	Great Man Theory	Trait Theory	Ohio State Leadership Theory	Fiedler's Contingency Model; Other Situational theories: Hollander; Hersey & Blanchard; House, Path-Goal	no one will dominate; multiple theories

Table 1.   Time-Line Overview of Leadership History

Another way of summarizing the history of leadership involves pointing out the locus of leadership, that is, delineating what has been the focus of study. Figure 6 depicts this.

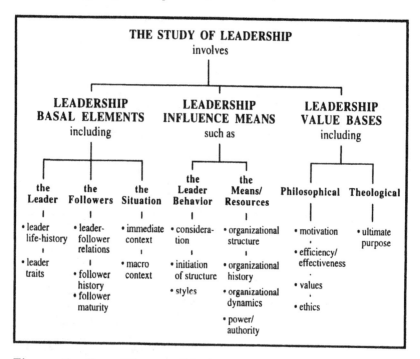

Figure 6. Tree Diagram Displaying Leadership Categories

In this diagram leadership styles is seen to be a major item under the element of leader behavior which in turn falls under the more generic category of Leadership Influence Means. Leadership Influence Means also includes organizational elements. Later I will mention the loose-tight organizational continuum and point out some implications for leadership style. For the present it is enough that one recognizes that Influence Means is complex and involves individual and corporate forces.

Historically, the study of leadership concentrated on the study of leaders in the Great Man Era, the study of traits of leaders in the Trait Era, the categorization of leader behaviors in the Ohio State Era, leadership styles and related factors in the Contingency Era and a variety of

Where it Fits in Leadership Theory

complex factors in the Complexity Era. Each era was a springboard into the next era.

In the Complexity Era, which followed Fiedler's Contingency Era, Hersey has done some creative thinking which expands leadership style theory. I shall discuss further Blake and Mouton, Fiedler, and Hersey in Section III of this paper which views various positions on leadership styles. It is enough for now that you have a quick grasp of the overview of the history of leadership theory and can see where leadership styles fits in that history. From the mid-fifties until the present, leadership styles have been a concern of leadership theory. Fiedler did the most to focus attention on leadership style as a major concern of leadership theory. Hersey has done more to communicate leadership style theory to the grassroots of leadership.

III.

Some Various Positions

A. Introduction

In this section I will first summarize some findings from Ray Downey's significant doctoral paper, "Church Growth and Leadership Styles: Implications for Ministerial Formation in Zaire," written in 1982. I will then go on to discuss three important style theorists: Mouton-Blake, Fiedler, and Hersey-Blanchard. These three style theorists are important since they approach leadership styles with very different presuppositions and hence arrive at different style theories and applications. Finally, I shall mention a Christian leader, Norman Shawchuck, who is a style theorist and applying style theory to pastoral work.

B. Some Observations From Downey

Ray Downey, a Christian and Missionary Alliance missionary to Zaire, did outstanding doctoral research in the area of leadership training. Downey was interested in training Zairian pastors and missionaries. He was particularly interested in spiritual formation and experiential training. In his research on training for Zairian pastors for church growth roles, he investigated Wagner's "strong-leader thesis."[14] He stated Wagner's thesis as follows.

> The "strong-leader" thesis is a principle of church growth articulated best by Dr. C. Peter Wagner of Fuller Theological

---

[14] The thrust of Downey's tutorial was to explore and challenge Wagner's idea of a strong leader as being necessarily only a task-oriented leader. In the Zairian context the majority of leaders would be relationship oriented (a strong cultural value) rather than task oriented. How to train church-growth pastors in that cultural context requires a serious evaluation of Wagner's thesis.

Seminary. In his book, **Your Church Can Grow**, he identified it as one of seven "vital signs" of a growing church in the Anglo-American context. Simply stated, it affirms that a church has good growth potential when it is led by a dynamic pastor who has the ability to motivate his entire congregation for growth. More recently in an article in **Leadership**, Wagner reaffirmed his observation, noting that "research has indicated that the potential for church growth increases, as the leadership role of the pastor increases, and the leadership role of the congregation decreases (1981:68). It will be necessary to identify what is meant by a "strong leader" both in the Anglo-American context and in the Zairian context. This will enable one to clarify the role of ministerial formation in providing the climate in which such leaders can be shaped and nurtured. (1982:2, 3)

Downey, in exploring the relation of a pastor's leadership style to the growth of his church, first reviewed leadership style taxonomies. His review encompassed both social science theorists and Christian leaders. He listed some 11 models relating to leadership styles. Table 2 summarizes Downey's survey results.

Some Various Positions 25

Type of Theorist	Model
Social Science Taxonomies[15]	
1. Max Weber (1957)	Three Ideal Types of Legitimate Authority
2. Kurt Lewin (1939)	Lewin's Triangle of Leadership Styles
3. Clarence Browne (1958)	Continuum of Leader Group Control
4. Fred E. Fiedler (1977)	Leader Match Model
5. Walter A. Hill (1973)	Hill's Four Leadership Styles
Christian Leader Taxonomies	
1. Richards & Hoeldtke (1980)	Church Leader's Role in Headship
2. Ted Engstrom (1976)	Five Leadership Styles
3. Bruce Powers (1979)	"Life Giving" Leadership Grid
4. Carl George (1980)	Catalyzers, Organizers & Operators
5. Arthur Adams (1978)	Authoritative-Participative Continuum
6. J. R. Clinton (1982)	Ten Biblical Leadership Styles

Table 2. Some Leadership Taxonomies

One of the weaknesses of Downey's research was his failure to include Hersey and Blanchard's situational leadership theory which adds the dimension of follower maturity. Had Downey studied that approach undoubtedly his findings on Zairian pastors and their leadership styles among their people would have been greatly enriched. Most likely he would not have opted as strongly for Fiedler's theory as he did. However, Downey's study is a good study. Before deriving the heuristic model which he used to analyze the Zairian pastoral situation, Downey summarized four observations from his taxonomic survey of this background study on leadership styles which I quote below (1982:21-23).

 1. *Directive/non-directive continuum.* Most of the taxonomies
    view leadership styles as being either directive or non-

---

[15] Numbers in parentheses refer to dates of publications from which Downey drew information. I have included these sources in the bibliography.

directive. Sometimes this is referred to as the "autocratic-democratic" continuum. Since both styles have proven effective in fostering church growth, our model has chosen not to give undue prominence to the directive/non-directive element.[16]

2. *Low/high concern for personhood continuum.* At least fifty percent of the taxonomies considered a leader's concern for personhood as being an important factor in determining his/her leadership style. Implicit in all leadership styles identified by Clinton is the leader's concern for personhood. Powers' "life-giving" leadership ideal is always characterized by a high concern for others, even though such leaders can vary between a high or low control of others (1979:26). It would seem that an ideal leadership style for a "church growth" pastor would also necessitate a high concern for others.

3. *Task-motivated/relationship-motivated continuum.* Closely related to the concern for personhood continuum is the task/people-motivated continuum. The Least Preferred Coworker (LPC) Scale used by Fiedler identifies a leader's style as being either task-motivated or relationship-motivated. Richards' headship models suggest that the command model is task-oriented whereas the sharing and servant models are people oriented. The managerial grid has as its horizontal axis the degree of concern for production which is essentially a task-oriented/people-oriented continuum. Pastors who are successful in leading their congregations into growth are generally task motivated even though they maintain a high concern for people. This factor will be examined further when the Heuristic Model is presented.

4. *Need for flexibility.* All of the Christian researchers, with the exception of Richards and Hoeldtke,[17] emphasize the

---

[16] This statement, particularly the implication that a democratic approach has brought church growth, needs confirming data which Downey does not give. This directly refutes Wagner's assertion.

[17] They advocate a servanthood approach to perception of role and to practice of leader behavior as the only biblical leadership style. Their approach, in my opinion, is

Some Various Positions

need for leadership style flexibility. This idea is also shared by the majority of the social scientists surveyed. Some of their comments are noted below.

> It is obvious that competent leaders will use a mixture of strategies. The particular blend of the authoritative and the participative in a given situation will depend on the views and the habits of the leader and the elements in the situation (Adams 1978:56).
>
> Leadership style varies yet the faith factor is common to all (Amstutz 1976:97).
>
> ... No one style of leadership behavior is always more appropriate than any other style and ... successful behavior is contingent upon the situation itself (Hill 1973:63).
>
> To be most effective, the leader should be able to adapt his style of leadership to the people and the environment in which he operates (Kilinski and Wofford 1973:78).
>
> It is quite possible that the apostle Paul made use of all the leadership styles identified by Clinton, adapting his style to the situation he faced. His leadership demonstrated that he was multi-styled. However, most leaders do not have the ability to quickly change their leadership style to fit the situation. Fiedler (1977:152:ff) suggests that it is probably much easier to change the situation.... (Downey, 1982:22, 23)

Points 1 and 4 above are both worth highlighting for our purposes. Downey was able to clearly identify various uses of the directive/non-directive continuum in most of the materials he surveyed. Of particular help was his analysis of Hill's research. Hill's research was helpful in demonstrating that leaders can be multi-styled in their leadership

---

strongly influenced by democratic ideals and a facilitator approach to the biblical concept of plurality of leadership. This could be a carry-over from the thrust of the sixties in which ideal leadership was trained in seminaries as facilitator leadership (strongly dependent on democratic ideals.)

approaches, but his generic categories overarching specific leadership styles were particularly helpful to me. Downey summarized Hill as shown in Figure 7 which follows.

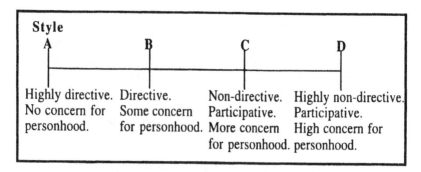

Figure 7. Model 6: Hill's Four Leadership Styles (Downey 1982:12)

When Downey applied this directive/non-directive thinking to my own analysis of biblical leadership styles (see section VI of this paper)[18] he further modified the generic categories above. The categories became Highly Directive, Directive, Non-directive, and Highly Non-directive. When he grouped my ten biblical styles along this continuum (which I had not done) I saw the value of a dual generic/specific category approach to leadership styles. That is, I now use the modified four-fold generic categories as an umbrella (and apply it first when analyzing a leader's style) under which I locate specific leadership behaviors typical of given leadership acts. This was a significant breakthrough for me in coming to my own definitions on leadership style. I rely more heavily on point 4 above concerning flexibility than Downey does.

Downey relied heavily on Fiedler's work in deriving his heuristic model which he used to analyze Zairian leadership styles. His eight conclusions concerning the Zairian situation and leadership styles, particularly in his modified view of Wagner's "strong leader" theory, are instruc-

---

[18] My ten styles analyzed by Downey have since been altered slightly. I dropped the servanthood style and split the father style into two component types. The new listing also orders the styles in light of Downey's continuum analysis.

tive for missiological leaders who are interested in designing training that will produce effective church growth pastors.[19]

C. Three Differing Views of Leadership Style Theory

In order to understand these three differing style approaches, Mouton-Blake, Fiedler, and Hersey-Blanchard, it is first helpful to see them in terms of the paradigmatic era in which they arose and to get the flavor of contingency models. I will discuss this background first and then discuss each of these three major approaches.

1. Background

Stogdill's watershed article in 1948 forced a paradigm shift from a direct focus on study of leaders (Great Man and Trait Theory) to what leaders do—their behavioral functions. The Ohio State and Michigan studies reduced leadership behavior to two basic generic categories—consideration and initiation of structure. How leaders did these two basic functions became the focus of the next period of leadership research, which I titled the Contingency Era. Leadership style was the topic which described those fundamental ways leaders operated. At the heart of all contingency theory lies the concept of leadership styles. Figure 8 seeks to categorize contingency models in terms of style assumptions.

---

[19] Since Downey's conclusions have proven helpful to many leaders in non-western cultures, I include them here for reference. In brief summary form Downey's eight conclusions (1982:32–36) are:
  (1) Recognize the difficulty of changing a person's leadership style.
  (2) Concentrate on changing the leadership situation, recognizing "ministerial formation" as one tool.
  (3) Select and train task-motivated leaders for planting new churches.
  (4) Give prominence to the training of men and women who are actually involved in ministry. [As opposed to those anticipating future ministry—my interpretive remarks—author]
  (5) Train people who demonstrate spiritual authority.
  (6) Give opportunity for younger candidates to intern with Zairian pastors who have a proven track record in church growth.
  (7) Use successful Zairian pastors as resource persons in Church Growth Seminars.
  (8) Encourage pastors to make use of laymen who are gifted "celebration" leaders.

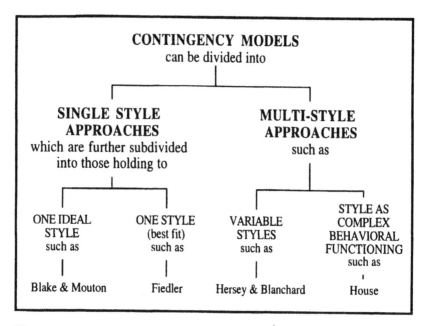

Figure 8. Advocates of Various Contingency Models in Terms of Style Approach

Table 3 summarizes several theorists, their contingency models, and the basic issues involved.

Theorist	Model	Basic Issue Involved
Blake & Moulton	Managerial Grid	The ideal leadership style is very high in relationship and very high in task. All leaders should strive for this style.
Fiedler	Contingency	A leader's style is related basically to his/her personality and thus can not be changed easily. Hence, one must either adjust the situation to fit that dominant style or change the leader to a situation for which his/her style functions best.
Hersey & Blanchard	Situational	Style is a function not only of situation but also of follower maturity. Different styles are optimally related to different follower maturity levels. A leader can be trained to use a multi-style which fits situation and follower maturity.
House	Path-Goal	Style is contingent on means of influencing toward goals

Table 3. Comparison of Style Theorists

Models which see leadership as a dynamic process involving leaders, followers, leader-follower relationships, task and other situational variables fall into the category called "Contingency Models".[20] I define a contingency model, as the label describing leadership theories which see leadership effectiveness as contingent upon leadership styles, followers and situational variables. The first model which actually went by this name was Fiedler's Contingency Model but the concept of leadership as a process which is contingent on more than just the leader or his/her traits or his personality was broader then just Fiedler's Model.

---

[20] Appendix A contains detailed definitions relating to contingency theory.

Let me give a quick overview of the three approaches before giving a more detailed look at each.

Concurrent with Fiedler's earliest research, Blake and Mouton had devised a model called the Managerial Grid as early as the mid-fifties which indicated that leadership effectiveness was directly proportional to a best leadership style which integrated a high task focus with a high relationship focus. Fiedler and others held that leaders had styles which were directly a function of personality and hence could not be altered easily. Therefore, for Fiedler effective leadership was contingent on discovering a leader's style and matching it to situational variables in which that style was most effective. Hersey and Blanchard, like Blake and Mouton, believed that leaders could be trained to utilize different styles, but unlike them, saw various styles as optimally related to various combinations of follower and situational variables.

2. One Ideal Style—Blake and Mouton's Approach—See Appendix A

In the mid-1960s Robert R. Blake and Jane S. Mouton published their book, **The Managerial Grid**. In it was a diagram called "The Managerial Grid," which was a display along an x-y axis. The y axis described "concern for people". It was scaled from 1 (low concern for people) to 9 (high concern for people). The x axis described "concern for production." It was scaled from 1 (low concern for production) to 9 (high concern). While not being exactly the same, these two variables were closely related to "consideration" and "initiating of structure" of the Ohio State model and "task" and "relations" of Fiedler's model. On the diagram were plotted five basic orientations that a leader could have to express how concern for production and concern for people were joined. Mouton and Blake make it clear that though people seem to be predisposed to manage in one way or another, the points on the Grid are not to be thought of as personality types that isolate a given individual's behavior. Identification on the Grid does not slot a person in a rigid and inflexible way. Behavior is flexible and can be changed.

I describe the managerial grid as a leadership theory which relates the integration of concern for production with concern for people into five basic clusters, each having basic assumptions which will influence leadership style. It advocates the high concern for people and the high concern for task cluster as the optimum leadership style for effectiveness.

Some Various Positions

Mouton and Blake asserted that managerial effectiveness in organizations is optimum when using a leadership style representing the 9, 9 plot. Some key assumptions of Blake and Mouton include:

a. A given individual's style may be viewed as flowing from a dominant set of assumptions, though there are backup assumptions which also influence the style.

b. These assumptions orient the leader as to thinking and behavior in dealing with production/people relationships.

c. Whenever a person's underlying managerial assumptions change, actual managerial practices also normally shift.

d. Any leader can accept new assumptions and change behavior accordingly.

e. A style, even a dominant one, is not fixed but varies as affected by the following elements: organization, situation, values, personality, chance.

f. Many styles are subject to modification via training.

3. One Basically Fixed Style—Fiedler's Approach

The most famous of the contingency models is Fiedler's. It has been most dominant throughout leadership study history in terms of generating discussion and research. It is one of the earliest and certainly best known of the situational theories of leadership. Briefly, Fiedler's Contingency Model sees effectiveness (where effectiveness is primarily performance toward organizational goals) as a function of matching one of two leadership styles (task-oriented or relations-oriented) with two kinds of general situations (favorable and unfavorable). Situational favorableness depends on three variables: leader-member relations, task structure and position power. Task-oriented leaders perform more effectively in very favorable and very unfavorable situations while relations-oriented leaders perform more effectively in situations intermediate in favorableness.

The model arose out of Fiedler's first major research. Fiedler, a psychologist by background, did early research which basically tried to predict leader effectiveness using a measure of leader attitudes called the LPC (least preferred co-worker). Essentially this was a trait approach to leadership. When he found different results for different kinds of leaders, he developed a contingency theory to explain the discrepancies. The model predicts that high LPC leaders, those with a motivational bias toward close interpersonal relationships, including subordinates, will perform more successfully in situations intermediate in favorableness. Low LPC leaders, with a bias toward achieving tasks, perform more successfully in very favorable and very unfavorable situations.

I describe Fiedler's Contingency Model as a leadership model which predicts effectiveness based on a leader's basic personality orientation toward achievement of task or relationships with followers and the leadership situation.

One strength of Fiedler's model is its strong assertiveness on predicting whether or not a given leader will produce well in a given situation. His predictions can be summarized as follows.

    a. Low (task oriented) LPC leaders perform better and run more effective groups when there is either very high or very low situational control (that is, the quality of leader-member relationships, the degree of task structure, and the position power of the leader are either altogether highly favorable or altogether highly unfavorable to the leader).

    b. High (relations-oriented) LPC leaders are most effective when there is intermediate situational control.

I describe some nine assumptions underlying this model. See Fiedler's Contingency Model in Appendix A. Of the nine, the key assumption for me is assumption 3: "A leader's style is a function of his/her personality and is basically fixed and falls dominantly into one of two styles (task oriented or relationship oriented)." It seems to me that this assumption, while generally true, can be challenged by findings of "transformational life-history" and by careful longitudinal study of leadership styles of biblical characters.[21]

4. Multi-Style Approach—Hersey and Blanchard's Situational Model

Another contingency model, one which moves more toward complexity models is Paul Hersey and Ken Blanchard's model (See Appendix

---

[21] Doohan (1984) implies such development over time in her analysis of Paul's leadership. My approach to the specific case study of leaders, called Transformation Life History, arrives at this conclusion also.

Some Various Positions

A for a detailed definition of this model). Hersey and Blanchard predict that the more managers adapt their style of leader behavior to meet the particular situation and the needs of their followers, the more effective they will tend to be in reaching personal and organizational goals. They define style as "... the behavior pattern that a person exhibits when attempting to influence the activities of others as perceived by those others" (Hersey & Blanchard 1982:95–96). A second quote gives their views on leader's abilities to have different styles and no one best style—issues on which they differ with Fiedler and Mouton/Blake. "In summary, empirical studies tend to show that there is no normative (best) style of leadership. Effective leaders adapt their leader behavior to meet the needs of their followers and the particular environment. If their followers are different, they must be treated differently. Therefore, effectiveness depends on the leader, the follower(s), and other situational variables; $E = f (l, f, s)$. Therefore, anyone who is interested in his or her own success as a leader must give serious thought to these behavioral and environmental considerations" (1982:103).

I describe their situational model as a multi-style leadership model which advocates that as leaders vary styles and appropriate power bases according to follower maturity, effectiveness increases. Their model necessitates a focus on the evaluation of followers and the development of followers. Their model is complex and is based on an interplay among (1) the amount of guidance and direction (task behavior) a leader gives; (2) the amount of socio-emotional support (relationship behavior) a leader provides; and (3) the readiness (maturity) level that followers exhibit in performing a specific task, function or objective.

5. Summary of the Three Approaches

Both Mouton-Blake and Fiedler developed single-style approaches, but they differ markedly. Mounton-Blake hold to an ideal style, one in which a leader in influencing followers holds an equally high regard for production and a high regard for people. They would assert that style is not fixed by personality and that leaders can change their behavior by changing their values regarding concern for production and concern for people. Fiedler would say that most leaders have a dominant style of leadership which is part of their personality. Further, certain styles are more effective in certain situations, a factor not admitted to by Mouton and Blake who see only one "good style." Fiedler would say then that style can not be changed readily. He would assert that because it can not be changed readily, it is easier to control the other variables affecting leadership, namely situation. If situation cannot be changed then shift the leader to a situation which matches his style.

Hersey-Blanchard would agree with Fiedler that different styles are effective in different situations. They would assert that Mouton-Blake's one ideal style is effective in certain situations, but is not effective in others. The new factor introduced into leadership style theory by Hersey-Blanchard is the concept of regulating leader style according to follower maturity as well as other situational variables. They see training as effective in changing leadership styles, changing situations, and changing followers' maturity. In fact, they see effective leadership as being highly concerned with using leadership styles which will develop followers toward higher maturity.

In brief then,

Mouton-Blake	hold that the ideal leadership style is very high in relationship and very high in task. All leaders should strive for this style.
Fiedler	holds that a leader's style is related basically to his/her personality and thus can not be changed easily. Hence, one must either adjust the situation to fit that dominant style or change the leader to a situation for which the style functions best.
Hersey-Blanchard	hold that leadership style is a function not only of situation but also of follower maturity. Different styles are optimally related to different follower maturity levels. A leader can be trained to develop a multi-style which fits situation and follower maturity.

6. Shawchuck's Emphasis

Norman Shawchuck, a management consultant to religious organizations operating out of Boise, Idaho, has seen the importance of applying leadership style theory to church situations. His article, "Are You A Flexible Leader?" reveals that his approach falls theoretically along Hersey-Blanchard's lines. In that article he shows how current problems in church situations are often a problem relating fundamentally to leadership style. I would agree. My own observations in parachurch organizations are that there is a sizable backdoor in leadership circles. That is, a number of promising leaders leave organizations. Now there are many reasons why this is so. But certainly one of them has to do with leadership styles of leaders over these promising potential leaders. I mention Shawchuck[22] here not for his theoretical contributions to leadership style, but to hold him up as an example of one in the Christian field who sees the importance and necessity of applying leadership style theory to Christian leadership—a conviction I also highly regard.

7. Where To Now?

How to resolve the thinking of these experts who have research to back up their resultant theories! That's the problem before us. I don't think the answer is an either/or type approach, but rather an acceptance of major ideas of all of them in an eclectic fashion. For leadership style theory is complex and one can find situations where any of the three theories applies, and situations contradicting any of the three. In the next section I give my eclectic synthesis to leadership styles.

---

[22] I suggest you read Shawchuck's article (1983). Then if you are interested in his analysis of leadership style, write: Organizational Resources Press, 2142 Oxnard Drive, Illinois, 60515. Ask for "Taking A Look At Your Leadership Styles," or "Taking Another Look At Your Leadership Styles."

IV.
Toward Definitions

A. Introduction

I personally believe that leadership style is a dynamic concept and not a static concept. To say that a person has such and such a leadership style is to use static thinking. It is to freeze forever one's opinion of a given leader's approach to influencing people. I believe that leaders utilize differing leadership styles depending on numerous factors. While it may be true that a given leader repeatedly uses a given leadership style in a variety of leadership acts, I prefer to talk about a given leadership act and the style that was used in that act. I also prefer to recognize a variety of styles or nuances of the same style where these can be seen. With this bias in mind I shall proceed to define three labels which I use to help me ascertain leadership style: situational leadership style, leadership style bent, dominant leadership style.

B. Situational Leadership Style

While it is much more difficult to fix a leader's style since leaders influence in a variety of situations with different styles, it is possible to analyze any given situation where influence is exerted and to describe the style for that given situation.

> definition: The *situational leadership style* of an individual is the behavioral pattern that a leader exhibits when attempting to influence the attitude and actions of followers in a given leadership act.[23]

---

[23] "Leadership act" is a term defined in the syllabus for the ML500 Introduction to Leadership Course. A *leadership act* is the specific instance at a given point in time of

A given leadership act can be evaluated with some certitude in terms of analysis of a leadership style.

C. Leadership Style Bent

Even those who hold to a multi-style leadership style theory agree that a given leader will usually prefer a given leadership style.[24] This tendency to prefer a certain favorite style I refer to as leadership style bent.

> definition: The *leadership style bent* of a leader is the dispositional tendency that a leader has, either toward task behavior or relationship behavior due to personality or cultural factors which affect the leader's situational leadership style.

Fiedler utilizes his least preferred co-worker (LPC) measurement to indicate this style bent. He ties it strongly to personality with the resulting implication that for most purposes it is relatively fixed. Mouton and Blake tie this "Predisposition to manage in one way or another" to a dominant set of assumptions which are subject to modification through formal instruction or self-instruction.[25] Hersey uses style profiles which he measures with LEAD PROFILES.[26] However you measure it, there seems to be a tendency within leaders toward giving priority either to task or relationships.

---

the leadership influence process between a given influencer [person said to be influencing] and follower(s) [person or persons being influenced].

[24] Hersey, whose situational leadership theory certainly embraces a multi-style approach, says this.

> Research at the Center for Leadership Studies has discovered that most leaders have a *primary* leadership style and a *secondary* leadership style. A leader's primary style is defined as the behavior pattern used most often when attempting to influence the activities of others. In other words, most leaders tend to have a favorite leadership style. (Hersey and Blanchard 1977:233)

[25] That is the thrust of **The Managerial Grid**. See pages 12–14 which explain Mouton and Blake's views of factors which affect this predispositional bent: assumptions, organization, situation, values, personality, chance.

[26] See Hersey and Blanchard, pages 247–264, which describe their approach to analysis of preference for styles. Their analysis is in terms of a primary and secondary style preference. They show the various combinations of style profiles.

Toward Definitions

D. Dominant Leadership Style

A comparative study of various leadership acts will most likely reveal that a given leader tends to influence in a given situation and for a given type of leadership function in a preferred way. When a given leadership style is seen to happen repeatedly in the majority of leadership acts, we can identify a dominant leadership style. We could use different weightings for the various functions depending on which are exercised more frequently or which are considered higher in a priority of leadership functions. In any case, we could assess a dominant and secondary (or tertiary, etc.) style if we had enough leadership acts to analyze to form some reliable data base. I define very generally, then, a dominant leadership style, and use it with caution because of my preferred bias for leadership style as a dynamic concept.

definition: The *dominant leadership style* of a leader is that

- highly directive or
- directive or
- non-directive or
- highly non-directive

consistent behavior pattern that underlies specific overt behavior acts of influence pervading the majority of leadership functions in which that leader exerts influence.

It may be that a comparative study of leadership acts may not reveal a dominant pattern. That would certainly be in line with my view of the dynamic concept of style. And even where a dominant pattern can be observed, one must remember that the factors influencing leadership style are themselves dynamic so that the dominant pattern may not hold. One must be aware of the tendency to view leadership style as a static concept which is inherent in the definition itself.

1. Directive—Non-Directive Continuum

I use the continuum described by Downey which views leadership influence as highly directive (leader centered action) to highly non-directive (follower centered). Along this continuum one can arrange various categories of styles depending on how a given author defines styles.

I use those four categories—highly directive, directive, non-directive, or highly non-directive—and relate them to Hersey and Blanchard's categories.[27]

> Highly Directive = S1 (telling)
> Directive = S2 (selling)
> Non-Directive = S3 (participating)
> Highly Non-Directive = S4 (delegating)

Figure 9. Hersey and Blanchard Categories Equated to Directive Categories

Later after talking about some biblical observations on Paul's leadership style in which I identify ten styles: apostolic, confrontation, father-initiator, father-guardian, obligation-persuasion, maturity appeal, imitator, nurse, consensus, and indirect, I will roughly associate them with Hersey and Blanchard's four major continuum positions as follows.

---

[27] See Hersey and Blanchard pages 152–155 for the descriptions of these terms: telling, selling, participating, delegating. See also pages 247–256 which describe various style profiles using combinations of these terms.

2. Relating Hersey and Blanchard to Biblical Styles

Hersey and Blanchard Categories	Pauline Categories
Highly Directive = S1 (telling)	apostolic, confrontation
Directive = S2 (selling)	father, obligation-persuation, maturity appeal
Non-Directive = S3 (participating)	imitator, nurse, consensus
Highly Non-Directive = S4 (delegating)	indirect

Figure 10. Biblical Styles Equated to Hersey and Blanchard and Directive Scales

E. Four Major Factors Influencing Leadership Style

I have mentioned that I see leadership style as a dynamic concept. I say that because I see leadership style varying due to a number of factors. While there may be several factors which actually determine how in a given leadership act a leader will influence, I have selected four which I believe should be considered when viewing a Christian leader and his/her leadership style. These four include leadership personality bent, leader function, follower maturity and leader-follower relation. Written in notational form then,

1. Functional Notation

Leadership styles = function (L_{per}, L_{fn}, F_{mat}, L-F_{rel}) where

L_{per} = leader personality bent

L_{fn} = leader function

L_{mat} = follower maturity

L-F_{rel} = leader-follower relationship

Now let me explain briefly each of these factors.

2. Leadership Personality Bent (L_{per})

Frequently in missiological circles it is suggested that missionaries from the West are often task oriented while nationals (particularly from Africa) are said to be relationship oriented.[28] While a blanket generalization like this cannot hold for missionaries and nationals it does point out the observed tendency for leaders to be task oriented or relationship oriented in their basic attitude toward accomplishing leadership functions.

The Ohio State studies were observation studies of what leaders actually did. They reduced numerous leadership functions to two major kinds of functions: 1) consideration and 2) initiation of structure.[29] These can be roughly equated with relationship behavior and task behavior.

Mouton and Blake suggest that leaders should seek to have awareness of these two major kinds of functional groupings. They assert that one

---

[28] The thrust of Downey's tutorial was dealing with this apparent difference as applied to Zairian leadership. Wagner's thesis plainly opts for strong leadership to bring about church growth, which implied that it be task oriented. Downey's struggles were to find out if strong leadership could be relationship oriented. And if so, could that kind of strong leadership see church growth.

[29] Halpin and Winer, in a now famous research study, used factor analysis to show that consideration and initiation of structure were in fact two independent variables. Fleishman recaptures the excitement of that early finding. Halpin and Winer's original study was written up in a paper published in 1952. A second account of the factor analysis approach which led to the findings of independent variables was published in 1957. I have listed that bibliographic entry.

The definitive study which identified consideration and structure was the Air Force project in which the questionnaires were administered to Air Force crews who described their aircraft commander (Halpin and Winer, 1952). I can still recall the excitement as Ban Winer, using a hand calculator, applied the Wherry-Winer iterative method of factor analysis to the item data. Much discussion ensued regarding the interpretation of the two major and two minor factors which appeared, and many suggestions were offered. The *consideration* factor seemed to be the easiest one to name and, I believe, it was John Hemphill who thought of the term *initiating structure* or *initiation of structure* to name the second factor.

The definitions of these factors which emerged were as follows: *consideration* seemed to involve behavior indicating friendship, mutual trust, respect, a certain warmth and rapport between the supervisor and his group.... *Initiating structure* seemed to involve acts which imply that the leader organizes and defines the relationships in the group, tends to establish well defined patterns and channels of communication and ways of getting the job done.

I recall what appeared to be at first puzzlement, followed by a real experience of insight when we had discovered these to be independent dimensions of leadership and not opposite ends of a single continuum (1973:7,8).

Toward Definitions

could, by a change of value systems and assumptions, assert leadership functional behavior which could optimize both task and relationship behavior (they used terminology of "concern for production" and "concern for people" as phrases which were roughly equated to initiation of structure and consideration). In fact, they stated that "high concern for people" with a simultaneous "high concern for production" was the optimum best managerial style.

Fiedler observed that in practice leaders usually had a dominant tendency toward either task behavior or relationship behavior. He asserted that this tendency was tied to personality. He further asserted that since it was tied to personality it was relatively unchangeable.[30] Hence his approach to leadership styles was to evaluate style and then put the person in a situation that "best fits" that dominant style.

It has been Hersey's experience that some people are rather fixed in their style bent but that many can alter assumptions and values and thus alter their leadership style to fit situations. His theory has been popularized under the phrase, "the situational leader"—which is the title of his very popular book. While on the one hand agreeing somewhat with Blake and Mouton (that is, people can vary styles), he would agree with Fiedler that a given situation calls for a particular style. Hersey goes on to talk about style range and style adaptability. "*Style range* indicates the extent to which leaders are able to vary their style; *style adaptability* is the degree to which they are able to vary their style appropriately to the demands of a given situation. . ." (Hersey and Blanchard:234).

In my true eclectic fashion I tend to agree somewhat with Fiedler and Hersey. My own observations of Christian leadership point out that many leaders are indeed rather inflexible and hence would not have a broad style range nor style adaptability. Yet I do see in other leaders (and in the scriptures themselves) a flexibility which allows for change of what I call leader personality bent. My feeling is that if a leader is flexible in general then he/she can be trained to alter leadership styles. I have a premonition that as a leader becomes older and gains more experience

---

[30] Fiedler does not say that personality cannot be changed but that it takes a good bit of time to do so and is not easy to do. Relatively speaking it is much easier to change the task, or other situational variables like leader-member relations. Hence, training thrusts should be on identifying a given style, and teaching how to change the situational factors to fit that style or transferring the person to another situation for which his/her style is optimum.

there is a tendency toward flexibility-inflexibility inertia. That is, leaders who are flexible early on can increase their flexibility while leaders who are rather rigid early on will tend to become more inflexible. Hence, I see that an important training goal for leadership is to expose leaders as early as possible to the concept of "flexibility testing" and to prepare them toward an openness about flexibility.

Now I am optimistic that God can change or at least modify personality bents. While it may be true that our culture or personality or both shapes us toward a task orientation or relationship orientation, God can reshape or modify us. No one seems to be born with servanthood as a controlling attitude for leadership functions. Nor do many cultures shape toward servanthood as a significant value for leadership thinking. Yet the Bible asserts that this attitude must be basal in a Christian leader. Hence it can be learned or developed within leadership. If this basic leadership value can be changed by God's transforming process, then other values toward task or relationship behavior can also be modified or used for God's purposes. Figure 11 sums up what I am saying in this paragraph. In the figure I am suggesting that though we may have a bent toward task or relationship which may be a personality thing or culturally induced thing, we must have a foundational attitude underlying it that is based on servanthood values. This is an acquired trait (attitude) which we see increasingly in our lives via the ministry of the Holy Spirit.

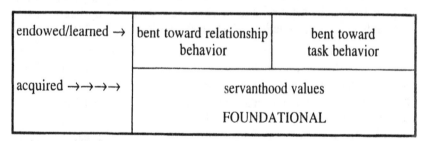

Figure 11. Relationships Between Major Personality Bent Factors

I suggest that in terms of assessing a given leader's personality bent an Inflexibility-Flexibility continuum be used first in a general sort of a way. That is, a leader should be evaluated in terms of flexibility for a number of previous leadership acts. Flexibility will be seen in terms of

Toward Definitions

style range and style adaptability, as well as the ability to change attitudes and plans in light of varying situations.

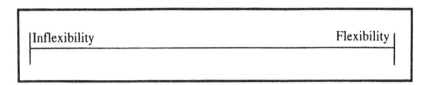

Figure 12. Inflexibility-Flexibility Continuum

This can be done for leadership acts specifically and for leadership functions generally. (See next section describing leadership functions). Where a given leader is located toward the inflexibility side of the continuum, I would suggest a Fiedler-approach toward leadership style. Where a given leader is located toward the flexible side of the continuum, I would suggest a Hersey-approach toward leadership style. These are summed up in the following suggestions:

Suggestion 1. *If high inflexibility, either engineer situation to fit the leader personality style or move leader to a situation more appropriate to that style.*

Suggestion 2. *If high flexibility, leader can be trained to learn skills and attitudes to offset personality bent and improve style range and adaptability.*

The leadership personality bent is probably the dominant factor affecting a given leadership style.

3. Leader Function (L_{fn})

Note again the leadership style functional notation

Leadership styles = function (L_{per}, **L_{fn}**, F_{mat}, L-F_{rel})

I have discussed the first and probably the most important factor, L_{per}. Now let me say also that leadership style not only varies according to personality bent but also varies in terms of the leadership function being exercised. I suggest that there are some basic leadership functions that most leaders participate in. Leadership styles will vary in the performance of these various functions. It is unreasonable to expect that one leadership style will dominate each of these functions. I will first suggest some generic categories that should most likely apply to all Christian leaders. Then I will suggest that each leader will have unique categories of leadership functions.

Leaders in general are responsible for the following generic categories of leadership functions.

Consideration Functions (relationship behaviors)
Christian leaders,
- must continually be involved in the selection, development and release of emerging leaders.
- are continually called upon to solve crises which involve relationships between people.
- will be called upon for decision making focusing on people.
- must do routine people-related problem solving.
- will coordinate with subordinates, peers and superiors.
- must facilitate leadership transition—their own and others.
- must do direct ministry relating to people (extent depends on giftedness).

Initiation of Structure Functions (task behaviors)
Christian leaders,
- must provide structures which facilitate accomplishment of vision.
- will be involved in crisis resolution which is brought about due to structural issues.
- must make decisions involving structures.
- will do routine problem solving concerning structural issues.
- will adjust structures where necessary to facilitate leadership transitions.
- must do direct ministry relating, maintaining, and changing structures (extent depends on giftedness).

Toward Definitions

Inspirational Functions (motivating toward vision)
Christian leaders,
- must motivate followers toward vision.
- must encourage perseverance and faith of followers.
- are responsible for the corporate integrity of the structures and organizations of which they are a part.
- are responsible for developing and maintaining the welfare of the corporate culture of the organization.
- (especially higher level) are responsible for promoting the public image of the organization.
- (especially higher level) are responsible for the financial welfare of the organization.
- are responsible for direct ministry along lines of giftedness which relate to inspirational functions.
- must model (knowing, being and doing) so as to inspire followers toward the reality of God's intervention in lives.
- have corporate accountability to God for the organizations or structures in which they operate.

4. Follower Maturity (fmat)

Let me give you the notational equation once again in order to refresh your memory in terms of the various elements affecting leadership style.

Leadership styles = function (L_{per}, L_{fn}, **F_{mat}**, L-F_{rel})

Having already looked at the first two factors, let's consider the third: follower maturity. It should be clear that leadership style will vary with the level of maturity of followers. That is, highly directive behavior will most likely be needed with immature followers while highly nondirective behavior will be more appropriate with very mature followers. Not all would agree with these assumptions. However, I think they generally hold true. But again I must caution that the other factors affecting leadership style may take priority. I see maturity as the ability and willingness of a follower to take responsible action in terms of a leadership task. For someone to do this it will require ability and willingness. Hersey and Blanchard describe these two ideas under the following maturity labels: job maturity and psychological maturity. I am weakest in this whole concept of follower maturity—especially in terms of what the Bible says about it and how that maturity correlates with leadership styles. But I sense that a follower's maturity should play a big factor in how a leader behaves to influence that follower. I sense that intuitively this is how Jesus operated in his training of the disciples over the three years that he worked with them. But I admit I need some concrete examples from the Bible to back this up.

I should mention that follower maturity is a major factor in Hersey and Blanchard's approach to leadership styles. Loren I. Moore, an advocate of Hersey and Blanchard's approach, has done specific doctoral and post-doctoral research on the measurement, assessment and evaluation of follower maturity.[31]

Even though I cannot at this time offer proof, other than referring you to Hersey and Blanchard's theory in general, I suspect that Christian leadership study needs to be especially conscious of follower maturity and of its potential effect on leadership style. The thrust of the Ephesians 4:7–16 leadership passage is on the responsibility of training followers in functions and maturity. Somehow these important leadership tasks must correlate with leadership style—that is, the behaviors leaders use to accomplish the tasks.

5. Leader-Follower Relationship (L-F_{rel})

For a final time let me set before you the notational form of leadership style and some major functions affecting it.

Leadership styles = function (L_{per}, L_{fn}, F_{mat}, **L-F_{rel}**)

I have discussed all but the final one, L-F_{rel}. It is my opinion that leadership style will vary according to the level of intimacy between leaders and followers. In the business world, leader-follower relationships are often specified in terms of allowable distance and intimacy. But Christian leadership differs. Christian leaders not only lead, and hence are different from the followers in the leadership responsibility, but they

---

[31] See "Toward the Determination of Follower Maturity: An Operationization of Life Cycle Leadership." Unpublished Doctoral dissertation. See also "The FMI: Dimensions of Follower Maturity" in **Group Organizational Studies**, 1976, 1, 203–222.

Toward Definitions 51

are also an intimate part of the group being led by virtue of their relationship to Christ as described in the body metaphor in Scripture. So that in living out the Christian life, leaders model their lives openly before followers and participate jointly in many functions which involve a deepened level of intimacy. This kind of intimacy must directly affect leadership styles that are used between Christian leaders and followers.

I suggest that in considering leadership style, a continuum which forces one to think of level of intimacy should be used. Where levels of intimacy between followers and leaders is distant, then organizational authority will be related to the power base from which the leader operates. This will show up in the leadership style used to influence. Where the leader-follower relationship moves toward the intimate side of the continuum, much less formal power bases related to spiritual authority will be reflected in leadership styles (and roles) used to accomplish leadership functions. These ideas are suggested in Figure 13 given below.

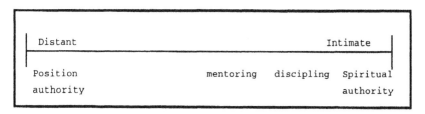

Figure 13. Leader-Follower Relationship Continuum

Let me summarize what I am trying to indicate in this discussion of leader-follower relationships.

observation: The level of intimacy affects use of leadership style. Intimacy is usually much higher in spiritual leadership than in secular leadership and will thus affect leadership style.

6. Summary of Leadership Factors Affecting Leadership Style

Leadership style will vary according to a number of factors. I have selected four which Christian leaders should consider.

The most difficult to deal with is the leadership personality bent which reflects itself in a leadership style bent, one of my three concepts I defined at the beginning of this section of the paper. For the leadership personality bent is related to inherent personality traits as well as to cultural factors.[32] We often have not had much control over these factors. I have suggested that the effects of these factors can be somewhat overcome in the lives of those who are relatively flexible. Relatively flexible people can most likely be trained in leadership style theory and will most likely be able to broaden style range and adaptability. Thus they will be useful in a variety of leadership roles and tasks. People who are less flexible can have very effective ministries also, but will have to be very careful to correlate their leadership styles to situations which are amenable to those styles.

It is when one carefully analyzes a variety of actual leadership functions such as motivation toward vision, decision making, crisis resolution, problem solving, development of leaders (selection and training), etc. that one will see indeed there probably is a style range in most leaders. It is helpful to be aware that different functions will require different style approaches.

Follower maturity is at this stage in my own understanding the most illusive of the factors affecting leadership style. What does follower maturity mean for people involved in churches and para-churches? In organizations where people are paid to do work, it is easy to see that job maturity and psychological maturity are important factors in carrying out a job. But it is much less clear in church and para-church organizations what maturity means. For church and para-church organizations must be concerned with total maturity of a person, that is, growth into Christian maturity which involves more than just skills, readiness or willingness to do a task. It is intricately bound up with "beingness" and transformation into the image of Christ. So then, while I sense that leadership style must vary in order to recognize and to develop maturity in a Christian follower, I do not yet have a clear idea of the relationship.

Styles will change according to leader-follower intimacy. It is clear from observing Paul's leadership style with various followers or follow-

---

[32] My own strong feeling from observation but without an assessment of data is that leadership styles of types A and B (that is local leadership in churches and para-church organizations) will correlate strongly to the dominate style of leadership seen in the surrounding culture by leaders functioning at equivalent levels.

er groups that intimacy level (as well as leader function) had a strong bearing on his leadership style. With intimate followers such as Titus and Timothy, Paul could use a highly directive style when the situation called for rapid action. In fact, with intimate followers Paul could use just about whatever style he wanted to. Not so with other followers or follower groups.

So then, a given leader's leadership style is probably not nearly so fixed as we would at first assume. It will vary—and should vary—due to a variety of factors, of which the four stressed above will be extremely important. A first step in altering or adapting leadership style is to recognize how it is affected by various factors.

V.
Steps in Style Analysis

I think it is helpful for any leader or emerging leader to study leadership style theory and to seek to ascertain his/her own leadership style. Table 4, above, is a first attempt at analyzing one's style. It approaches leadership style primarily from a self-analysis viewpoint.[33]

Step	General Procedure	Detailed Suggestions
1.	LIST LEADERSHIP FUNCTIONS	1. List generic function. 2. List specific functions.
2.	LIST STYLES FOR EACH	1. It is probably easier to do specific first. List specific behaviors that you use to influence in each of these specific functions. 2. For each behavior you list seek to identify it generally under the generic categories of highly directive, directive, non-directive, highly non-directive. 3. Repeat detail suggestions 2 and 3 for generic leadership functions in which you participate.

---

[33] I am aware of Hersey's definition of leadership style. "... the style of leaders is the consistent behavior patterns that they use when they are working with and through other people *as perceived by those people.*" [italics mine]. I believe that self-analysis is valid as well as analysis of others—Hersey's emphasis. Hersey also recognizes the validity of self-analysis. His whole section on the Johari window shows the need for discrepancy analysis. I prefer to have a leader analyze his/her own leadership style and for the functions where valid feedback from followers can be given to use discrepancy analysis. A person's leadership style is both that which he/she perceives as well as that perceived by the followers.

Step	General Procedure	Detailed Suggestions
3.	DETERMINE DOMINANT STYLE	1. Using whatever priority you feel appropriate for your leadership functions (both generic and specific), determine the total number of highly directive, directive, non-directive, and highly non-directive styles you use. 2. For whatever weighting system you use, calculate your dominant style.
4.	DETERMINE SECONDARY STYLE	1. Calculate your second most dominant style.
5.	EVALUATE TWO-STYLE PROFILE	1. Use Hersey and Blanchard to help you understand the potential strengths and weaknesses of your style profile. 2. Remember the various other factors that affect style. The analysis by Hersey and Blanchard may need to be modified due to these other factors.
6.	DISCREPANCY ANALYSIS	1. Where possible, that is, for styles that are directly seen and/or understood by followers, seek to get confirmation of denial of your own analysis of your leadership style. 2. It may prove helpful for you to read the section in Hersey and Blanchard on the Johari Window in order that you may better understand the need for discrepancy analysis.
7.	ANALYZE GROWTH POTENTIAL	1. Use flexibility continuum. 2. Analyze potential for growth in style range and adaptability. 3. Make growth plans *or* contingency plans. (Either do situational engineering or move into new situation with better fit.)

Table 4. 7 Step Analysis of Leadership Styles

Here is an alternative approach to step 2.

| 2. | USE GENERALIZED COMMERCIAL TESTING IN LIEU OF SELF-TESTING. | 1. Take Hersey's Lead Test.[34]
 2. Use Fiedler's LPC.[35]
 3. Use Shawchuck's Test.[36] |

---

[34] Hersey's Lead Test is available through:
Learning Resources Corporations
8517 Production Avenue
P.O. Box 26240
San Diego, California 92126

[35] Fiedler's test is available with his book **Improving Leadership Effectiveness: The Leader Match Concept**, revised edition. It is co-authored with Martin M. Chemers and Linda Majar. It was published by John Wiley and Sons, Inc.

[36] Norman Sawchuck gives a simplified test along with his article, "Are You A Flexible Leader," which appeared in **Leadership**, Spring 1983. I am sure that other more complicated tests are available. The article gives an address where Shawchuck can be reached.

VI.
Observations on Pauline Leadership Styles

Leadership style, as we have seen in Section IV, deals with the individual behavioral expression a leader utilizes in influencing followers. This individual expression includes methodology for handling crises, methodology for problem solving, methodology for decision making, methodology for coordinating with superiors, peers and subordinates, methodology for handling leadership development. The individual methodology for a specific leadership act or series of acts can often be labeled as well as identified on the Directive—Non-Directive continuum. Primarily we are interested in the four categories on the continuum since we are seeking to identify a primary/secondary style profile. But it is also very helpful when we can give labels to the specific influence behaviors.

Sometime in the past I studied Paul's methods of working with and influencing followers as best I could identify them from his letters. I labeled ten styles with specific labels. While we do not have conclusive data to state these with absolute authority, the styles certainly suggest that Paul was multi-styled in his approach to influencing followers. The styles are not defined exclusively. That is, there is some overlap of concepts between different styles. Let me describe the ten styles I labeled. Later I will come back and comment on Helen Doohan's appraisal of Paul's leadership.

A. Ten Pauline Styles Observed

1. Apostolic Style

Where a person demonstrates with self-authenticating evidence that he/she has delegated authority from God—that is, there is a sense of spiritual authority about the leadership—then that person can use the apostolic leadership style.

definition: The *apostolic leadership style* is a method of influence in which the leader
- assumes the role of delegated authority over those for whom he/she is responsible,
- receives revelation from God concerning decisions, and
- commands obedience based on role of delegated authority and revelation concerning God's will.

A synonym for this style is the command/demand style. This style is implied in I Thessalonians 5:12, 13. "And we beseech you, brethren, to know them which labour among you, and are over you in the Lord, and admonish you; and to esteem them very highly in love for their work's sake." It is implied in I Timothy 5:17: "Let the elders who rule well be counted worth of double honour, especially they who labour in the word and doctrine." Another example implying this style is seen in Hebrews 13:17: "Obey them that have the rule over you, and submit yourselves: for they watch for your souls, as they that must give account, that they may do it with joy and not with grief; for that is unprofitable for you." This style is also seen in I Thessalonians 2:6; even though Paul chooses not to command obedience, he asserts that he could have done so as was his apostolic right. The essence of the apostolic style is the legitimate right from God to make decisions for others and to command or demand their compliance with those decisions.

This style with its top-down command/demand approach is considered the most highly directive leadership style.

2. Confrontation Style

Many leaders try to avoid problems, particularly those involving troublesome people and those carrying heavy emotional ramifications. The basic rationale seems to be, "this is a tough problem; if I try to do anything about it I'm going to incur wrath, maybe have my character maligned, lose some friends and be drained emotionally. Perhaps if I just ignore it, it will go away by itself." For some problems, perhaps this is a good philosophy; time does give opportunity for a clearer perspective, for healing, and for indirect conflict to occur. But for most problems, leaders must confront the problem and parties involved directly. At least this seems to be the approaches exemplified in Jude, John, Peter, and Paul in their Scriptural writings.

> definition: The *confrontation leadership style* is an approach to problem solving
> - which brings the problem out in the open with all parties concerned,
> - which analyzes the problem in light of revelational truth,
> - and which brings force to bear upon the parties to accept recommended solutions.

This style is usually seen in combination with other styles. Seemingly, the majority of cases emphasize *obligation-persuasion* as the force for accepting the solution, but *apostolic* force is also seen in the Scriptures. The book of Jude is an example. Several of the leadership acts in the book of First Corinthians utilize this style. Paul utilizes this style in the Philippian church. See the problem between Euodia and Synteche. For some help in this area of leadership style see David Augsburger's book published by Regal Books, **Caring Enough To Confront**.

This style, like the apostolic style, is highly directive since the solutions to the problems are often the leader's solutions.

3. Father-Initiator Style

Paul resorts to this leadership style when exerting his influence upon the Corinthian church. He is establishing his authority in order to suggest solutions to some deep problems in the church.

> definition: The *father-initiator leadership style* is related to the apostolic style which uses the fact of the leader having founded the work as a lever for getting acceptance of influence by the leader.

I Corinthians 4:14, 15 Paul writes: "I write this to you, not because I want to make you feel ashamed, but to instruct you as my dear children. For even if you have ten thousand guardians in your Christian life, you have only one father. For in your life in union with Christ Jesus, I have become your father by bringing the Good News to you." Paul uses the father-initiator style in this case. Note in this example the force of the two powerful figures:[37] the absolute for the relative in verse 14 and the hyperbole in verse 15.

The father-initiator style is closely related to the obligation-persuasion style, in that obligation (debt owed due to founding the work) is used as a power base. However it differs from obligation-persuasion in that more than persuasion is used. The decision to obey is not left to the follower. It is related to the apostolic style in that it is apostolic in its force of persuasion.

This style is highly directive/directive style.

4. Obligation-Persuasion Style

One method of influencing followers over which you have no direct organizational control involves persuasion. The leader persuades but leaves the final decision to the follower. A particularly powerful technique of persuasion is obligation-persuasion in which normal appeal techniques are coupled with a sense of obligation on the part of the follower due to past relationship/experience with the leader. Such a leadership style is seen with Paul's treatment of the Onesimus/Philemon problem.

definition: An *obligation-persuasion leadership style* refers to an appeal to followers to follow some recommended directives which

- persuades, not commands followers to heed some advice;
- leaves the decision to do so in the hands of the followers, but
- forces the followers to recognize their obligation to the leader due to past service by the leader to the follower;
- strongly implies that the follower owes the leader some debt and should follow the recommended advice as part of paying back the obligation; and finally
- reflects the leader's strong expectation that the follower will conform to the persuasive advice.

---

[37] See my book **Figures and Idioms** published by Barnabas Resources which defined these idioms and shows how to capture their emphatic meaning.

The classic example of this is illustrated in the book of Philemon. Paul uses this style in combination with other styles in First and Second Corinthians also.

This is a directive style. The expectation is high, though the actual decision to do so passes to the follower.

5. Father-Guardian Style

This style, much like the nurse style, elicits an empathetic concern of the leader toward protection and care for followers.

> definition: The *father-guardian style* is a style which is similar to a parent-child relationship and has as its major concern protection and encouragement for followers.

Usually this style is seen when a very mature Christian relates to very immature followers. I Thessalonians 2:10, 11 illustrates this style. "You are our witnesses, and so is God, that our conduct toward you who believe was pure, right, and without fault. You know that we treated each one of you just as a father treats his own children. We encouraged you, we comforted you, and we kept urging you to live the kind of life that pleases God, who calls you to share in his own Kingdom and glory."

Usually this style is directive, but because of the caring relationship between leader and follower and the follower maturity level it does not seem directive, since influence behavior always seem to have the follower's best interest at heart.

6. Maturity Appeal Style

The book of Proverbs indicates that all of life is an experience that can be used by God to give wisdom. And those who have learned wisdom should be listened to by those needing yet to learn. Maturity in the Christian life comes through time and experience and through God-given lessons (as well as giftedness—see word of wisdom gift, Clinton 1985). Leaders often influence and persuade followers by citing their "track record" (learned wisdom) with God.

> definition: A *maturity appeal leadership style* is a form of leadership influence which counts upon

- Godly experience, usually gained over a long period of time,
- an empathetic identification based on a common sharing of experience, and
- a recognition of the force of imitation modeling in influencing people in order to convince people toward a favorable acceptance of the leader's ideas.

Hebrews 13:7 carries this implication: "Remember your former leaders who spoke God's message to you. Think back on how they lived and died and imitate their faith."

See also 1 Peter 5:1-4, 5-7 where Peter demonstrates maturity appeal. "I who am an elder myself, appeal to the church elders among you. I am a witness of Christ's sufferings, and I will share in the glory that will be revealed. I appeal to you to be shepherds of the flock that God gave you and to take care of it willingly, as God wants you to, and not unwillingly. Do your work, not for mere pay, but from a real desire to serve. Do not try to rule over those who have been put in your care, but be an example to the flock. And when the chief Shepherd appears, you will receive the glorious crown which will never lose its brightness."

Paul's description of his sufferings as an Apostle (II Corinthians 11:16-33) and experience in receiving revelation (II Corinthians 12:1-10) are exemplary of the maturity appeal style leadership.

This style moves between the categories of directive to non-directive depending on how forcefully the desired result is pushed for.

7. Nurse Style

In 1 Thessalonians 2:7 Paul uses a figure to describe a leadership style he used among the Thessalonian Christians. The figure is that of a nurse. It is the only use of this particular word in the New Testament, though related cognates do occur. The essential idea of the figure is the gentle cherishing attitude of Paul toward the new Christians in Thessalonica with a particular emphasis on Paul's focus on serving in order to help them grow.

> definition: The *nurse leadership style* is a behavior style characterized by gentleness and sacrificial service and

loving care which indicates that a leader has given up "rights" in order not to impede the nurture of those following him/her.

The primary example is given in I Thessalonians 2:7, "But we were gentle among you, even as a nurse cherisheth her children." Paul commands an attitude of gentleness to Timothy in 2 Timothy 2:24–25. "And the servant of the Lord must not strive, but be gentle unto all men, apt to teach, patient, in meekness, instructing those that oppose him, if God perhaps will give them repentance to the acknowledging of the truth."

The nurse style is similar to the father-guardian style in that both have a strong empathetic care for the followers. It differs in that the father-guardian style assumes a protective role a la a parent to child. The nurse role assumes a nurturing focus which will sacrifice in order to see nurture accomplished.

The nurse style is non-directive.

8. Imitator Style

Paul seemed continually to sense that what he was and what he did served as a powerful model for those he influenced. He expected his followers to become like him in attitudes and actions. It is this personal model of *being* and *doing* as a way to influence followers that forms part of the foundational basis for spiritual authority.

> definition: The *imitator style* refers to a conscious use of imitation modeling as a means for influencing followers. It reflects a leader's sense of responsibility for what he/she is as a person of God and for what he/she does in ministry with an expectant view that followers must and will and should be encouraged to follow his/her example.

The Good News Bible captures Paul's emphasis in Philippians 4:9 which illustrates this leadership style. "Put into practice what you learned and received from me, both from my words and from my actions. And the God who gives us peace will be with you." A second Pauline illustration is seen in II Timothy 3:10, 11. "But thou hast fully known my doctrine, manner of life, purpose, faith, long-suffering, love, patience, persecutions, afflictions, which came unto me at Antioch, at Iconium, at Lystra, what persecutions I endured; but out of them all the Lord delivered me." Paul goes on to give the response he expects of Timothy based on this imitation modeling and maturity appeal.

Larry Richard's, in his book **A Theology of Christian Education**, points out this methodology of influence as being one of the most powerful tools a leader can use to influence followers. Secular theory also points out this methodology as very important. (cf. Bandura 1962, 1977.)

This style is highly non-directive.

9. Consensus Style

Decisions which affect people's lives and for which leaders must give account require careful spirit-led consideration. One leadership style approach to decision making involves consensus decision making. This style is often used in coordination situations where ownership is desired. Cultures which stress group solidarity, such as many of the tribes in Papua New Guinea, see this style used frequently by leaders.

> definition: *Consensus leadership style* refers to the approach to leadership influence which involves the group itself actively participating in decision making and coming to solutions acceptable to the whole group. The leader must be skilled in bringing diverse thoughts together in such a way as to meet the whole group's needs.

In a consensus style there is much give and take in arriving at decision. Unless there is a "check in the spirit" which prohibits an agreement, the final decision carries the weight of the entire group and thus will "demand" all to follow through on implications and ramifications which follow. James apparently gives a consensus decision reflecting the entire group's corporate will in the Acts 15 decision. Note this decision was identified as Spirit-led. The Acts 6 decision concerning distribution of good to widows is an example of both of consensus (within the plurality of Apostles) and apostolic (commanded to the followers) leadership styles.

This style is highly non-directive.

10. Indirect Conflict Style

A powerful style for dealing with crises and problem solving involves the concept of dealing with "first causes," that is, the primary motivating factors behind the problem rather than the problem itself. This style recognizes that spiritual conflict is behind the situation and must be dealt with before any solution will take hold. The parties directly involved may not be aware that the leader is even doing problem solving. A leader who uses this approach must be skilled in prayer, understand spiritual warfare and either have the gift of discerning spirits or access to a person with that gift.

> definition The *indirect conflict leadership style* is an approach to problem solving which requires discernment of spiritual motivation factors behind the problem, usually results in spiritual warfare without direct confrontation with the parties of the problem Spiritual warfare is sensed as a necessary first step before any problem solving can take place.

See the context of Matthew 16:21–23 especially verse 23: "Get away from me Satan. You are an obstacle in my way, because these thoughts of yours don't come from God, but from man." This is an example of indirect conflict leadership style. Mark 3:20–30 gives the underlying idea behind this style. See especially verse 27: "No one can break into a strong man's house and take away his belongings unless he first ties up the strong man; then he can plunder his house." See also Ephesians 6:10–20, especially verse 12: "For we are not fighting against human beings but against the wicked spiritual forces in the heavenly world, the rulers, authorities, and cosmic powers of this dark age."

This style is highly non-directive.

B. Doohan's Observations On Pauline Leadership

In an insightful book which demonstrates familiarity both with secular leadership theory and biblical leadership concepts, **Leadership in Paul**, Helen Doohan analyzes Paul's leadership via a longitudinal approach. That is, she studies Paul's leadership over an extended time period beginning first with his earlier ministry and progressing through to his latter ministry.

She brings to her analysis an excellent knowledge of secular theory such as Hersey-Blanchard's situational leadership perspectives. And she uses the many secular perspectives in a heuristic manner to stimulate what she sees in the text. She studies Paul's early leadership by analyzing the first letter to the Thessalonians (and comparing it to the second). She studies Paul's approach to conflict and confrontation in the letter to the Galatians. She analyzes Paul's response to division and diversity in the Corinthian letters. She sees his growing maturity in the Roman epistle. She traces his maturity in leadership to its final conclusion in her analysis of the letter to the Philippians.

In all of her analyses she offers sharp insights into leadership perspective and principles. Here are a few sample remarks taken from her final chapter titled, "Conclusion: Paul the Leader."

> A leadership person who utilizes a variety of approaches is clearly identified in the correspondence. Paul is a powerful example of a religious leader, and offers a perspective on leadership that withstands the test of time. There are key insights into the appropriate exercise of leadership for the committed Christian who must deal continually with crisis, challenge, development and change. (Doohan 1984:165)

Here are some comments taken from her "Implications and Reflections" section of that final chapter.

> Although there is no best leadership style and no best strategy for change, the most effective leaders adapt and augment their responses according to environmental and situational demand. Likewise, there is no ideal leader or leadership approach. Rather, leadership is an interactional response between leaders and followers in various and unique situations. While this assessment is certainly true for Paul, his religious convictions consistently determine the parameters and the quality of his response. He has experienced the Lord, and he has a Christian vision of life. In the contemporary church, the exercise of Christian leadership should integrate acceptable and effective leadership approaches with religious values. Leadership styles must be consistent with a personal and corporate religious identity. Paul is a model and an exemplar in the sphere of religious leadership.

Observations on Pauline Leadership Styles

Paul's leadership was significantly affected by the followers he encountered. The dynamics between these two entities can be dramatic and forceful. Responsibilities are heavy on the part of both groups. In the contemporary church, persons in leadership positions are subject to an extraordinary amount of criticism and confrontation. While Paul offers insights into dealing with opposition, it must be noted that the most personally satisfying experiences and the deepest spiritual insights are evident in the communities in which mutual esteem, respect, support and affirmation exist. Today, leaders and followers are challenged to create this type of atmosphere so all persons can offer their real gifts to the church.

Finally, Paul's leadership effectiveness is not necessarily positively correlated with the amount of time he spends with individuals or with the communities. Corinth was his place of residence for a long period of time and the recipient of four letters from the founder of the church. Yet, the theological depth of Romans is not achieved in these letters, nor the revealing spirituality permeating the letter to the Philippians. Perhaps leisure and distance are essential ingredients if a maturity and refinement in leadership and vision are to be achieved. The "burned out" leaders of the church would do well to pause, to assess and integrate experience and theology. With an integrated leadership approach, a qualitatively different level of interaction and life will begin to emerge in the church. (Doohan 1984:166, 167)

Doohan's assessment of Paul as a multi-styled leader who matured as a leader confirms my own intuitive observations and does so from a systematic analysis of data. Where highly directive styles are called for because of the situation and maturity of followers, Paul uses them. Where participative highly non-directive styles are appropriate, Paul uses them. Paul varies his style according to situation, task, and level of maturity of followers.

I have offered this interlude on Doohan for four reasons.

1. I want to make you aware of this excellent work so that you might be encouraged to read it to learn about leadership. The book is valuable not only for the insights into religious

leadership and the principles seen in Paul's leadership but in its modeling.

2. This is an example of a scholarly credible work. It shows one doing serious biblical studies in leadership with a broad understanding of secular leadership theories as well as an intimate knowledge of scripture. I hope to challenge you and many others to do this same kind of scholastic work.

3. This book offers a methodology for studying leadership in the scriptures—she lays her framework for what religious leadership is, then she tells you her presuppositions on secular leadership theory, then she tells you how she will study Paul. Finally, she uses the same structure for analyzing each of the books: the situation, the issues, interaction and response, and assessment of Paul's leadership.

4. Finally, I mention Doohan's work because it confirms my own views of Paul's multi-style approach and progress in leadership maturity.

Doohan has done an outstanding job of analyzing Pauline leadership. And she has done it in a scholarly manner. I am challenged by her work and convinced that the Bible offers a gold mine for leadership theologizing by serious missiological researchers.

C. Summary of Lessons Biblical Styles

I think the following are worth noting because they point out what I have been attempting to do in this section dealing with biblical styles, most of which come from Pauline material.

1. I have demonstrated how to use the generic (directive/non-directive continuum) as the overarching umbrella on which to pinpoint specific leadership-style behaviors.

2. I have demonstrated how to look at specific behavior and identify it in terms of style. The ten definitive descriptions are models for doing this.

3. In identifying these ten models of specific styles seen in the Scriptures, I believe that most of them are transferable to many situations which we as leaders face today.

4. I have indicated that Paul's leadership style was multi-styled.
5. I have pointed out that Paul was a flexible leader who matured in his leadership as he grew older and was able to change to meet changing situations.

VII.

Miscellaneous Concepts Relating to Leadership Style

A. Introduction

There remain a few odds and ends pertaining to leadership style which I have not managed to work in so far. I will collect these odds and ends in this section. They pertain to the larger context in which leadership styles are exercised. Most writers on leadership styles assume strong organizational coherence. Therefore the application of leadership styles from most of these writers assumes power bases and power forms not always available to the Christian worker. Hence, I wish to point out that the coherence of organizational structure plays a vital part in power bases available to Christian workers, and hence highlights the place of individual power (especially spiritual authority). Where the organization is loose, individual power concepts will prevail. Where the organization is tight, organizational power concepts will swing into play. And where organizational coherence is tight, pressure from corporate organizational life styles will have force in determining leadership styles.

B. The Organizational Coherence Continuum

Organizations, whether secular or Christian, differ in their organizational coherence. By "organizational coherence" I mean the degree to which the organization is highly structured and defined in terms of initiation of structure functions. I use the Organizational Coherence Continuum to help me recognize this important point. In general, as you move from left to right along the continuum the coherence increases.

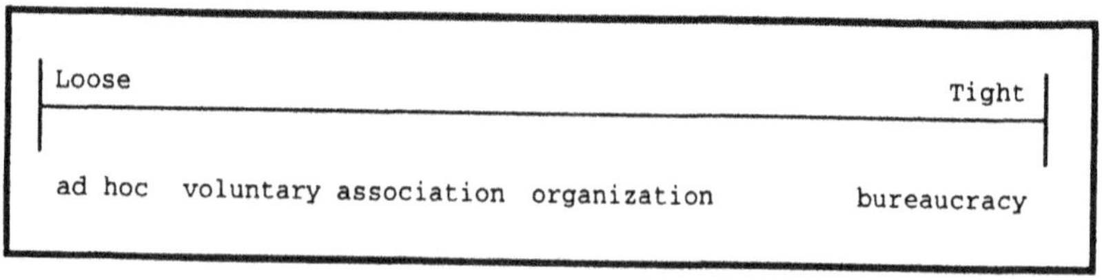

```
| Loose                                              Tight |
|                                                          |
| ad hoc   voluntary association   organization   bureaucracy |
```

Figure 14. Organizational Coherence Continuum

On the left end of the continuum there is much freedom for creativity in the organization. On the right creativity has to be channeled to fit the structure and controls of the organization or be lost. On the left there is little organizational power to move members toward accomplishment of tasks. On the right there is great power to force conformity on members.

Churches, especially small ones, are made up of organizations which fall more to the left of the continuum due to the voluntary nature of membership. As churches grow they move more to the right and will be composed of large staffs which operate organizationally along with voluntary members. Para-church organizations usually start out toward the left (but to the right of churches) on the continuum and move toward the right. Because they are so task oriented, structural coherence usually develops rapidly. There is a general trend for all organizations to move toward the right of the continuum.[38]

I am suggesting that as organizational coherence increases it will affect leadership styles in at least two important ways.

1. Organizational culture develops along with acceptable leadership styles for the organization. This puts pressure on individual leaders in the organization to conform to the accepted leadership styles and thus often limits a leader's ability to use a multi-styled situational approach to leadership.

---

[38] Larry Greiner's article, "Evolution and Revolution As Organizations Grow" in the **Harvard Business Review** points out this trend. Greiner is looking at business organizations and not churches or para-church organizations; nevertheless, his concepts apply somewhat to church and parachurch situations.

Miscellaneous Concepts Relating to Leadership Style   75

2. As one moves toward the right on the continuum more importance is given to organizational power as the influence means and lessens the use of individual power. The power bases and forms that can be used correlate to leadership styles that can be used.[39]

C. Power Concepts of Wrong and Mintzberg

Hersey and Blanchard devote two chapters to discussing leadership and power. One chapter, Chapter 8, "Situational Leadership, Perception, and the Impact of Power," correlates leadership styles with the most appropriate forms of power to use. This selection by Hersey and Blanchard should alert us to the vital role between power and leadership style.

Two very helpful writers on power include Dennis Wrong and Henry Mintzberg. Wrong looks at power in terms of individual relationships. He sees power in terms of a power holder, a power subject and the means the power holder uses to gain compliance from the power subject. Mintzberg is interested in power as it is seen in organizational contexts, that is, more than just individual power.[40] Let me suggest how I apply Wrong and Mintzberg's concepts in terms of the Organizational Coherence Continuum previously described.

---

[39] Hersey and Blanchard (1977) devote a whole chapter in their book to show how power forms and bases correlate to styles and maturity of followers. See chapter 8, "Situational Leadership, Perception, and the Impact of Power."

[40] See Appendix C which gives some ideas from Wrong and Mintzberg. Mintzberg's whole series of books are crucial for Type D and Type E leadership which must constantly deal with organizational dynamics. See footnote 41 for explanation of the leadership typology, A, B, C, D, E.

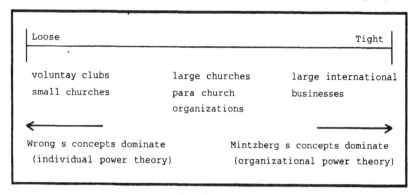

Figure 15. Wrong and Mintzberg Related to Organizational Coherence

I am suggesting that a leader who is vitally interested in his/her leadership styles should be concerned about power theory, for leadership style is a way of influencing followers. And influence means will require power. The looser the organization is, the more concepts from Wrong will be helpful in understanding the power behind the use of leadership styles. The tighter an organization is, the more Mintzberg's concepts on organizational power will come into play. Appendix C gives some introductory material on Wrong and Mintzberg. I leave further study of these important men to those who see the necessity of correlating power and leadership styles.

D. Some Final Suggestions on Power And Leadership Style

Because of the importance of power upon the whole influence process, and specifically upon the leadership styles of the power holder in a power situation, I believe it is vital for leaders to concern themselves with power theory. Therefore, I suggest the following as important follow-up suggestions to this section:

1. Study power (and its related concept of authority) in the Old and New Testaments so that you will have a firm base for understanding power—both its supernatural perspective and its natural perspective. Theorists like Wrong and Mintzberg look at power basically from a naturalistic view-

point. Particularly a Christian leader should have values concerning power and its use.
   2. Study Hersey and Blanchard's chapters which deal with Power: Chapter 5, "Determining Effectiveness," which relates power to effectiveness and Chapter 8, "Situational Leadership, Perception, and the Impact of Power."
   3. Study Wrong's definitions concerning power and power forms.
   4. Study Mintzberg's organizational power configurations in order to see the dynamics involved in power changes in an organization.

It is obvious to me that Christian leadership in general, and missiologists in particular, have not been active in researching leadership styles, particularly the relevance of these basically Western concepts. In my ministry abroad I have challenged missionaries and national leaders to study leadership style theory both for their own lives and to discover concepts particularly for type A and type B[41] leaders—those involved more specifically in grassroots ministry. We don't have facts. We cannot theorize cross-culturally without some data. So my fifth and final suggestion is

   5. Let's do some research on leadership style theory. In our own ministries, let's observe what is happening, write up our observations and publish to help others. Let's do research abroad at all levels along the leadership continuum (Types A, B, C, D, E). And let's write up our findings and pass them out to others so that all of us can benefit from the lessons and apply them to our own leadership.

---

[41] Type A leaders are leaders who work within local churches or small organizations (usually as volunteer workers). Type B leaders are leaders within that same context but whose functions bridge outside the organization (they may be unpaid or partially paid). Type C leaders are heads of churches whose leadership extends well beyond the local church or heads of small organizations who influence at local church levels. (They are fully paid "professional Christian workers.") Type D leaders influence at regional or national level. Type E leaders influence across several national situations.

Summary and Conclusions

At the beginning of this paper I mentioned that the thesis of this paper involved several assumptions. An understanding of leadership styles

1) requires historical analysis of the concept,
2) needs to be correlated with leadership theory as a whole,
3) became the focus of leadership theory during the Ohio State Era and the Contingency Era of leadership history,
4) points out the complexity involved in leadership influence,
5) is foundational to the training and development of leaders,
6) requires reflection from a Christian standpoint (most leadership style theory has come from secular leadership theorists),
7) is in need of further research from a missiological standpoint.

I pointed out that the structure of the paper was set up to develop or suggest the above ideas.

In Section I, I gave three reasons for studying leadership style.

1. A leader who wants to avoid unnecessary conflict needs to know about leadership styles.
2. Leaders aware of a variety of styles will use styles most appropriate to the developing of the followers.
3. Leaders should study leadership styles in order to expand capacity to lead—a strong biblical incentive for leaders.

While many reasons could be given, these three highlight personal growth and responsibility.

Section II dealt with points 1, 2, and 3 of my assumptions which all concern the historical background in which leadership style theory arose. Concepts are always best understood when seen in light of the times that prompted them. Leadership style theory developed out of the Behavior Era of leadership theory. Important people contributing to the study of leadership style include Mouton-Blake, Fiedler, and Hersey-Blanchard among many others. A proper understanding of leadership styles requires a broad knowledge of the theories associated with these important persons.

Sections III, IV, and V dealt either directly or indirectly with points 4 and 5, that is, those indicating the complexity of style theory and the need for leaders to know this theory in order to train others for effective ministry. Reference to Downey's work hinted at the large amount of background work that has been done in the leadership field which relates to leadership style theory. The most important concept noted in Downey's work was his use of the directive/non-directive continuum which I have applied in my own viewpoint on styles as the generic (umbrella) categories under which I identify specific leadership styles.

The emphasis on the three differing views of leadership style theorists—one ideal style, one fixed style, and multiple styles—also indicated the complexity of leadership style theory. All of these views contain important truth. I suggested that situations exist where each of these theories fail to explain what happens. I also suggested that situations exist where these theories will explain very well what is happening in the influence process. So I have opted for an eclectic approach to viewing styles.

My own definitions stress the importance of not stereotyping anyone as to a given leadership style but to recognize that styles vary with

1. personality bent
2. the situation, task or leadership function being performed
3. follower maturity
4. the leader-follower relationship (which is uniquely different for Christian leadership from secular leadership).

In dealing with situation and task or function I suggested that a leader could examine generic leadership functions as well as specific leadership functions when seeking to analyze his/her leadership style. I believe the

Summary and Conclusions

generic functions can help us to analyze the breadth of our view of leadership. I suggested that generic leadership functions, that is, categories of leadership functions that should be included in any Christian leadership situation include:

Consideration Functions (relationship behaviors)
Christian leaders,
- must continually be involved in the selection, development and release of emerging leaders.
- are continually called upon to solve crises which involve relationships between people.
- will be called upon for decision making focusing on people.
- must do routine people-related problem solving.
- will coordinate with subordinates, peers and superiors.
- must facilitate leadership transition—their own and others.
- must do direct ministry relating to people (extent depends on giftedness.

Initiation of Structure Functions (task behaviors)
Christian leaders,
- must provide structures which facilitate accomplishment of vision.
- will be involved in crisis resolution which is brought about due to structural issues.
- must make decisions involving structures.
- will do routine problem solving concerning structural issues.
- will adjust structures where necessary to facilitate leadership transitions.
- must do direct ministry relating maintaining and changing structures (extent depends on giftedness).

Inspirational Functions (motivating toward vision)
Christian leaders,
- must motivate followers toward vision.

- must encourage perseverance and faith of followers.
- are responsible for the corporate integrity of the structures and organizations of which they are a part.
- are responsible for developing and maintaining the welfare of the corporate culture of the organization.
- (especially higher level) are responsible for promoting the public image of the organization.
- (especially higher level) are responsible for the financial welfare of the organization.
- are responsible for direct ministry along lines of giftedness which relate to inspirational functions.
- must model (knowing, being and doing) so as to inspire followers toward the reality of God's intervention in lives.
- have corporate accountability to God for the organizations or structures in which they operate.

I also gave my personal opinion that leaders, by the grace of God, can change basic personality bents which can open them up to a wider range of styles. To further highlight my opinion on this point, I make reference to the servanthood value which is foundational to Christian leadership. I point out that the servanthood value is not a natural part of any leader's inherited personality bent or culturally determined style. It is learned only through growth as a Christian leader via the power of the Holy Spirit. I stress the importance of flexibility in this regard. Christian leaders should be people who are constantly growing in their flexibility both in their personal behaviors and in their ability to release emerging leaders under them.

Section VI discusses leadership styles in terms of scriptural observations. In that section I am seeking to show how to group specific influence behavioral patterns, that is leadership styles seen in given biblical leadership acts, under the umbrella concepts of the directive/non-directive continuum. I also am seeking to show how to identify and define spe-

Summary and Conclusions

cific leadership styles. I also show that Paul was multi-styled in his leadership influence. Some of the styles I defined can be directly transferred to Christian leadership today. All are worthy of study.

In that section I also introduce you to Helen Doohan, an outstanding Christian leader, who has analyzed Paul's leadership in a scholarly work which integrates secular and spiritual leadership perspectives. Her own analysis confirms my own, that leaders (even those with a strong task orientation as Paul had) can be multi-styled and need to be, in fact, in the complex situations that Christian leadership does today.

Section VII suggests that power is an important ingredient and should be studied by Christian leaders since it correlates so strongly with leadership styles. Wrong's theory on power which looks at power more abstractly in terms of individual power will apply to organizations which are loosely structured as so many Christian churches and para-church organizations are with their inherent volunteer membership. Mintzberg's organizational power theory will apply to those organizations which are more tightly structured as is the case with many denominations and older, larger para-church organizations.

Finally, let me close by saying that ministry flows out of being. What you are in terms of your character will reflect itself in your leadership style, your behavior patterns for influencing. You will need to be thoroughly familiar with biblical values which should permeate your leadership and hence be reflected in your leadership style.

Appendix A.

Contingency Theory Concepts

TWO CATEGORIES OF CONTINGENCY MODELS

introduction   Stogdill's watershed article (1948) forced a paradigm shift from a direct focus on study of leaders (Great Man and Trait theory) to what leaders do—their behavioral functions. The Ohio State and Michigan studies reduced leadership behavior research to two basic generic categories—consideration and initiation of structure. How leaders did these two basic functions became the focus of the next period of leadership research. Leadership style was the topic which described those fundamental ways leaders operated. At the heart of all contingency theory lies the concept of leadership styles.

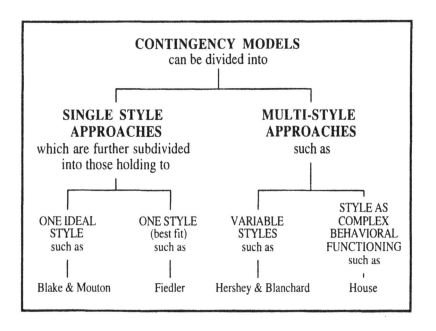

Theorist	Model	Basic Issue Involved
Blake & Moulton	Managerial Grid	The ideal leadership style is very high in relationship and very high in task. All leaders should strive for this style.
Fiedler	Contingency	A leader's style is related basically to his/her personality and thus can not be changed easily. Hence, one must either adjust the situation to fit that dominant style or change the leader to a situation for which his/her style functions best.
Hersey & Blanchard	Situational	Style is a function not only of situation but also of follower maturity. Different styles are optimally related to different follower maturity levels. A leader can be trained to use a multi-style which fits situation and follower maturity.
House	Path-Goal	Style is contingent on means of influencing toward goals

Appendix A. Contingency Theory Concepts

CONTINGENCY MODELS

introduction Models which see leadership as a dynamic process involving leaders, followers, leader-follower relationships, task, and other situational variables fall into the category called Contingency Models. The first model which actually went by this name was Fiedler's Contingency Model but the concept of leadership as a process which is contingent on more than just the leader, his traits or his personality was broader than just Fiedler's model. Blake and Mouton had devised a model, called the Managerial Grid, as early as the mid-fifties which indicated that leadership effectiveness was directly proportional to a best leadership style which integrated a high task focus with a high relationship focus. Fiedler and others held that leaders had styles which were a direct as function of personality and hence could not be altered easily. Therefore, for Fiedler, effective leadership was contingent on discovering a leader's style and matching it to situational variables in which that style was most effective. Hersey and Blanchard, like Blake and Mouton, believed that leaders could be trained to utilize different styles, but unlike them saw various styles as optimally related to various combinations of follower and situational variables. Other theories, like Hollander's Exchange Theory and House's Path Goal, were contingency theories in that they did not focus just on leader variables, but the heart of their theories relates only obliquely to leadership styles.

definition *Contingency Model* is the name given to leadership theories which see leadership effectiveness as contingent upon leadership styles, followers and situational variables.

example Fiedler's Contingency Model sees effectiveness (where effectiveness is primarily performance toward organizational goals) as a function of matching one of two leadership styles (task oriented or relations oriented) with two kinds of general situations (favorable and unfavorable). Situational favorableness depends on three variables: leader-member relations, task structure and position power. Task-oriented leaders perform more effectively in very favorable and very unfavorable situations, while relations-oriented leaders perform more effectively in situations intermediate in favorableness.

example Hersey and Blanchard's Life Cycle Model sees leadership effectiveness (where effectiveness is complex and primarily a measure of Likert's dependent variables: output variables [productivity/performance], intervening variables [the condition of the human resources] and short and long range goals) as a function of a leader altering various combinations of task and relationship behavior to that needed by follower maturity.

Appendix A. Contingency Theory Concepts

MANAGERIAL GRID

introduction   In the mid-1960's Blake and Mouton published their book, **The Managerial Grid**. In it was a diagram called "The Managerial Grid," which was a display along an x-y axis. The y axis described "concern for people." It was scaled from 1 (low concern for people) to 9 (high concern for people). The x axis described "concern for production." It was scaled from 1 (low concern for production) to 9 (high concern). While not being exactly the same, these two variables were closely related to "consideration" and "initiating of structure" of the Ohio State Model and "task" and "relations" of Fiedler's Model. On the diagram were plotted five basic orientations that a leader could have to express how concern for production and concern for people were joined. Mouton and Blake make it clear that though people seem to be predisposed to manage in one way or another, the points on the Grid are not to be thought of as personality types that isolate a given individual's behavior. Identification on the Grid does not slot a person in a rigid and inflexible way. Behavior is flexible and can be changed.

description   *The Managerial Grid* represents a leadership theory which relates the integration of concern for production with concern for people into five basic clusters, each having basic assumptions which will influence leadership style. It advocates the high concern for people and the high concern for task cluster as the optimum leadership style for effectiveness.

prediction   Managerial effectiveness in organizations is optimum when using a leadership style representing the 9, 9 plot.

assumptions
1. Three organizational universals include: purpose, people, hierarchy.
2. Theories regarding managerial behavior can be identified according to how these three elements are related.
3. These theories represent sets of assumptions which describe how a given individual can manage.
4. A given individual's style may be viewed as flowing from a dominant set of assumptions though there are backup assumptions which also influence the style.
5. These assumptions orient the leader as to thinking and behavior in dealing with production/people relationships.
6. Leaders may not be aware of these assumptions.
7. Whenever a person's underlying managerial assumptions change, actual managerial practices also normally shift.
8. Any leader can accept new assumptions and change behavior accordingly.
9. A style, even a dominant one, is not fixed but varies as affected by the following elements: organization, situation, values, personality, chance.
10. Many styles are subject to modification via training.

further study See Blake and Mouton (1964).

Appendix A. Contingency Theory Concepts

FIEDLER's CONTINGENCY MODEL

introduction   The leadership theory which has been most dominant throughout leadership research history in terms of generating discussion and research has been Fiedler's Contingency Model. It is one of the earliest and certainly best known of the situational theories of leadership. Fiedler, a psychologist by background, did early research which basically tried to predict leader effectiveness using a measure of leader attitudes called the LPC (least preferred co-worker). Essentially this was a trait approach to leadership. When he found different results for different kinds of leaders, he developed a contingency theory to explain the discrepancies. The model predicts that high LPC leaders, those with a motivational bias toward close interpersonal relationships, including those with subordinates, will perform more successfully in situations intermediate in favorableness. Low LPC leaders, with a bias toward achieving tasks, perform more successfully in very favorable and very unfavorable situations.

description   *Fiedler's Contingency Model* is a leadership model which predicts effectiveness based on a leader's basic personality orientation toward achievement of task or relationships with followers and the leadership situation.

predictions   1. Low (task-oriented) LPC leaders perform better and run more effective groups when there is either very high or very low situational control (that is, the quality of leader-member relationships, the degree of task structure, and the position of power of the leader are either altogether highly favorable or altogether highly unfavorable to the leader).

2. High (relations-oriented) LPC leaders are most effective when there is intermediate situational control.

key words

LPC: (least preferred co-worker): a measure of the leader's basic personality/value orientation.

High LPC: leaders value interpersonal success.

Low LPC: leaders value task success.

Situational control: an analysis of the situation in which the leader and followers work as measured by three items: leader-member relations, task structure, position power.

Leader-member relations: a measure of the leader's influence leverage as related to personal power.

Task structure: a determination of how well defined the goals, operating procedures and evaluation procedures of the group are.

Position power: a measure of the leader's authority due to position in the organization to use coercive power to bring about compliance.

Appendix A. Contingency Theory Concepts

NINE ASSUMPTIONS UNDERLYING FIEDLER's CONTINGENCY MODEL

introduction While these may not be presuppositional assumptions underlying Fiedler's model, they are certainly important ones.

Nine Assumptions

1. Leadership effectiveness is essentially a measure of a group's goal performance as directed by a given leader.
2. Leadership effectiveness is dependent on the interaction of leadership style and situational favorableness.
3. A leader's style is a function of his/her personality and is basically fixed and falls predominantly into one of two styles (task oriented or relationship oriented.)
4. A leader's style can be measured.
5. The Least Preferred Co-worker (LPC) instrument measures leadership styles.
6. Situational favorableness, the degree to which the situation itself provides the leader with potential power and influence over the group's behavior, is operationally indexed along three component dimensions: leader-member relations, task structure, and position power. (Ashour 1973:340)
7. Leader-member relations assumption: A leader who has the loyalty and support of subordinates can depend on them to comply enthusiastically with his/her directions. On the other hand, a leader whose subordinates dislike (or at least disrespect) him/her has no referent power and must be careful that they do not ignore his/her directions or subvert his/her policies. (Yukl 1981:135) Three different measures have been used:

leader's rating of the group atmosphere, members' ratings of group atmosphere, and the degree to which the leader is sociometrically chosen. (Ashour 1973:340)

8. Task structure assumptions: A task is highly structured when there is a detailed description of the finished product or service, there are standard operating procedures that guarantee successful completion of the task, and it is easy for the leader to determine how well the work has been performed. (Yukl 1981:135) Scales for measuring include goal clarity, decision variability, salvation specificity and goal-path multiplicity. (Ashour 1973:340)

9. Position power assumption: When a leader has substantial position power, he/she is able to administer rewards and punishments to increase subordinate compliance with his/her directions and policies. Leaders with little or no position power must rely on other sources of influence of behavior (Yukl 1981:135).

comments   Fiedler has found that leader-member relations are the most important of the three determinants of situational control, followed next by task structure and finally position power. (Yukl 1981:135)

further study   See Ashour (1973), Yukl (1981), Bass (1981:343–357).

HERSEY AND BLANCHARD's SITUATIONAL MODEL
syn: Life Cycle Model

introduction The basic assumption of Hersey and Blanchard in their situational model is this: The more managers adapt their style of leader behavior to meet the particular situation and the needs of their followers, the more effective they will tend to be in reaching personal and organizational goals. They define style as "... the behavior pattern that a person exhibits when attempting to influence the activities of others as perceived by those others" (Hersey & Blanchard 1982:95–96).

They differ with Fiedler and Mouton/Blake in their view that studies do not indicate one normative or best style of leadership. Thus, a leader can utilize different styles, adapting to the needs of different followers and environments. Effectiveness depends on the leader, followers, and other situational variables; $E = f(l, f, s)$.

description *The Hersey-Blanchard Situational Model* is a multi-style leadership model which advocates that as leaders vary styles and appropriate power bases according to follower maturity, effectiveness increases.

comment Situational leadership is based on an interplay among (1) the amount of guidance and direction (task behavior) a leader gives; (2) the amount of socio-emotional support (relationship behavior) a leader provides; and (3) the readiness (maturity) level that followers exhibit in performing a specific task, function or objective.

further study See Hersey (1984); Hersey & Blanchard (1982).

Appendix B.

Supplementary Bibliography on Leadership Styles

Supplementary Bibliography on Leadership Styles

Aral, S. O., and Whelan, R. K.
    1974   **Leadership Styles in Urban Societies.** Tucson: Univ. of Arizona, Institute of Government Research.

Ashour, A. S.
    1973   "The Contingency Model of Leadership Effectiveness: An Evaluation." **Organizational Behavior and Human Performance.** 9, 339–335.

Bass, B. M. and Valenzi, E. R.
    1974   "Contingent Aspects of Effective Management Styles." (J. G. Hunt and L. L. Larson, Eds.), **Contingency Approaches to Leadership.** Carbondale: Southern Illinois University Press.

Bass, B. M., Valenzi, E. R., Farrow, D. L., and Solomon, R. J.
    1975   "Management Styles Associated with Organizational, Task, Personal and Interpersonal Contingencies." **Journal Applied Psychology,** 60, 720–729.

Blake, R. R., and Mouton, J. S.
    1964   **The Managerial Grid.** Houston: Gulf.

Boheber, M. E.
    1967   "Conditions Influencing the Relationships Between Leadership Style and Group Structural and Population Characteristics." **Dissertation Abstract,** 28, 776–777.

Clinton, J. R.
  1986   "Coming To Some Conclusions on Leadership Styles." Unpublished paper. Pasadena: SWM, Fuller Theological Seminary.

Csoka, L. S. and Bons, P. M.
  1978   "Manipulating the Situation to Fit the Leader's Style—Two Validation Studies of LEADER MATCH." **Journal Applied Psychology**, 63, 295–300.

D'Angelo, R. V.
  1973   "The Influence of Three Styles of Leadership on the Process and Outcome of an Organizational Development Effort." Doctoral Dissertation. University of California, Berkeley.

Dreilinger, et al
  1982   "Beyond the Myth of Leadership Style Training—Planned Organizational Change." **Training Development Journal**, 36, 70–74.

Fiedler, F. E., O'Brien, G. E., and Ilgen, D. R.
  1969   "The Effect of Leadership Style Upon the Performance and Adjustment of Volunteer Teams Operating in Successful Foreign Environments." **Human Relations**, 22, 503–514.

Filley, A. C., and Jesse, F. C.
  1965   "Training Leader Style: A Survey of Research." **Personnel Administration**, 28, 14–21.

Fodor, E. M.
  1976   "Group Stress, Authoritarian Style of Control, and Use of Power." **Journal Applied Psychology**, 61, 313–318.

Golembiewski, Robert T.
  1961   "Three Styles of Leadership and Their Uses." **Personnel**, 38, 34–45.

Appendix B. Supplementary Bibliography on Leadership Styles

Heller, F. A.
    1972   "Research on Five Styles of Managerial Decision Making." **International Student Management Organization**, 11, 85–104.

Hill, Walter A.
    1973   "Leadership Style: Rigid or Flexible?" **Organizational Behavior & Human Performance**, 9, 35–47.

Hollander, E. P.
    1966   "Leader Style, Competence, and Source of Authority as Determinants of Active and Perceived Influence." Buffalo: State University of New York, Technical Report.

LaGaipa, J. J.
    1969   "Biographical Inventories and Style of Leadership." **Journal of Psychology**, 72, 109–114.

McGregor, Douglas
    1960   **The Human Side of Enterprise**. New York: McGraw-Hill Book Company.

Shapira, Z.
    1976   "A Facet Analysis of Leadership Styles." **Journal Applied Psychology**, 61, 136–139.

Shawchuch, Norman
    1981   *How to Be a More Effective Church Leader*. Downers Grove, Ill: Spiritual Growth Resources.

Tannebaum, Robert and Schmidt, Warren H.
    1973   "How to Choose a Leadership Pattern." **Harvard Business Review**, May-June 1973.

Wagner, L. W.
    1965   "Leadership Style, Hierarchical Influence, and Supervisory Role Obligations." **Administration Science Quarterly**, 9, 391–420.

Willower, D. J.
    1960   "Leadership Styles and Leaders' Perceptions of Subordinates." **Journal of Educational Sociology**, 34, 58–64.

Yu, Danny Kwok Leung
    1975   **A Consideration of Leadership Style and Multiple Staff Ministry and their Implications for Unity Among Chinese Churches in North America.**

Appendix C.

Power Concepts of Wrong and Mintzberg

Power Concepts of Wrong and Mintzberg

Below are some concepts and insights concerning Dennis Wrong and Henry Mintzberg.

I. Concepts of Dennis Wrong

One of Wrong's most important works is the book, **Power—Its Forms, Bases, and Uses**, New York: Harper and Row, 1980. The thesis of that book given in terms of major thrusts and ideas developed around that thrust is as follows:

subject	POWER, as the capacity of leaders (power holders) to produce intended and foreseen effects on others (power subjects)
major idea 1	can be analyzed in terms of its major forms: force, manipulation, persuasion, authority, each of which can be further broken down into sub-categories and which focus on the power subject's compliance
major idea 2	but also can be analyzed in terms of its major bases: individual and collective resources which focus on the power holder's resources,
major idea 3	and ultimately is necessary wherever groups pursue collective goals.

On the following page is given the structure defining power forms as organized by Wrong (1980:24).

Tree Diagram Containing Wrong's Major Concepts

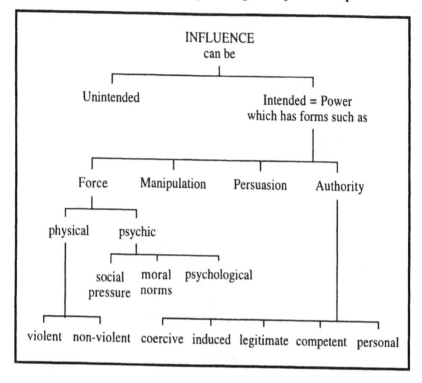

Some Important Definitions in Wrong's View of Power Theory:

Power is the capacity of some person (the power holder) to produce intended and foreseen effects on others (power subjects).

Three Attributes of Power Relations: Power is said to be *extensive* if the power subjects are many. Power is said to be *comprehensive* if the power holder's means of influence and variety of actions is considerable (i. e. the number of scopes in which the power holder controls the activities of the power subjects). Power is said to be *intensive* if the power holder can gain compliance of the power subject over a deep range, that is, within each scope the power holder has a range of effective options open to control the power subject.

Appendix B. Supplementary Bibliography on Leadership Styles

Manipulation: is any deliberate and successful effort by a power holder (A) to influence the response of the power subject (B) where the desired response has not been explicitly communicated to the power subject (B). (Wrong 1979:28)

Persuasion: is any situation in which A presents arguments, appeals or exhortations to B, and B, after independently evaluating their content in light of his/her own values and goals, accepts A's communication as the basis of his/her own behavior.

II. Concepts of Henry Mintzberg

Mintzberg has several very important books for those interested in leadership theory, particularly as it applies to organizations and organizational development or organizational dynamics. But the book most helpful to those interested in correlating power theory to leadership styles is **Power In and Around Organizations**. Englewood Cliffs, N. J.: Prentice-Hall, Inc., 1983.

Mintzberg defines *power* as the capacity to effect (or affect) organizational outcomes. (Mintzberg 1980:4) He looks at the major influencers in organizational power and defines an external coalition and an internal coalition. In each of these he very carefully defines the various actors in the power drama. Having defined each of the players in the game, he goes on to show the power configurations that normally exist in practice.

MINTZBERG's SIX POWER CONFIGURATIONS

External Coalition	Internal Coalition	Power Coalition
Dominated	Bureaucratic	The Instrument
Passive	Bureaucratic	The Closed System
Passive	Personalized	The Autocracy
Passive	Ideologic	The Missionary
Passive	Professional	The Meritocracy
Divided	Politicized	The Political Arena

Three of these power configurations—the Autocracy, the Missionary and the Bureaucratic—are frequently seen in church and in para-church organizations.

Bibliography

Bibliography

Adams, Arthur Merrihew
   1978   **Effective Leadership for Today's Church.** Philadelphia: The Westminster Press.

Amstutz, John Lee
   1976   **Church Growth in the San Fernando Valley: A Study of Three Churches.** Unpublished Doctoral Dissertation. Pasadena: Fuller Theological Seminary.

Bandura, A., Ross, D., and Ross, S. A.
   1962   **Vicarious Reinforcement and Imitation.** Unpublished manuscript, 1962a. Stanford, California: Stanford University.

Bandura, A.
   1977   **Social Learning Theory.** Englewood Cliffs: Prentice Hall.

Bass, Bernard
   1981   **Stogdill's Handbook of Leadership.** New York: The Free Press.

Blake, Robert R. and Mouton, Jane S.
   1964   **The Managerial Grid.** Houston: Gulf Publishing.

Browne, Clarence
   1958   **The Study of Leadership.** Danville: The Interstate Printers and Publishers, Inc.

Clinton, J. R.
1982   **Leadership Selection Models.** Unpublished Syllabus and Topic Notes. Pasadena: Fuller Theological Seminary.

Clinton, J. R.
1983   **Figures and Idioms.** Altadena: Barnabas Resources.

Clinton, J. R.
1984   **Leadership Emergence Patterns.** Altadena: Barnabas Resources.

Clinton, J. R.
1985   **Spiritual Gifts.** Beaverlodge, Alberta, Canada: Horizon House Publishers.

Doohan, Helen
1984   **Leadership in Paul.** Wilmington, Del.: Michael Glazier, Inc.

Downey, Raymur J.
1982   "Church Growth and Leadership Styles: Implications for Ministerial Formation in Zaire." Unpublished Doctoral Tutorial. Pasadena: School of World Mission, Fuller Theological Seminary.

Engstrom, Theodore Wilhelm
1976   **The Making of a Christian Leader.** Grand Rapids: Eerdmans Publishing Co.

Fiedler, F. E.
1967   **A Theory of Leadership Effectiveness.** New York: McGraw-Hill.

Fiedler, F. E., Chemers, Martin M. and Mahar, Linda
1977   **Improving Leadership Effectiveness: The Leader Match Concept.** New York: John Wiley and Sons, Inc.

Bibliography

Fleishman, E. A.
    1973   "Twenty Years of Consideration and Structure." (E. A. Fleishman and J. G. Hunt, Eds.), **Current Developments in the Study of Leadership.** Carbondale: Southern Illinois University Press.

George, Carl
    n. d.   Unpublished training materials for Fuller Evangelistic Association.

Greiner, Larry
    1972   "Evolution and Revolution As Organizations Grow." **Harvard Business Review**, July-August 1972 pp. 37–46.

Halpin, A. W. and Winer, B. J.
    1957   "A Factorial Study of the Leader Behavior Descriptions." (R. M. Stogdill and A. E. Coons, Eds.), **Leader Behavior: Its Description and Measurement.** Columbus: Ohio State University, Bureau of Business Research.

Hersey, Paul
    1984   **The Situational Leader.** New York: Warner Books.

Hersey, Paul and Blanchard, Kenneth S.
    1982   Management of Organizational Behavior—Utilizing Human Resources. Fourth Edition. Englewood Cliffs, N. J.: Prentice Hall.

Hill, Walter A.
    1973   "Leadership Style Flexibility, Satisfaction and Performance" (E. A. Fleishman and J. G. Hunt, Eds.), **Current Developments in the Study of Leadership.** Carbondale: Southern Illinois Press.

Kilinski, Kenneth K. and Wofford, Jerry C.
    1973   **Organization and Leadership in the Local Church.** Grand Rapids: Zondervan Publishing House.

Knowles, Malcolm
    1980   **The Modern Practice of Adult Education.** San Francisco: Josey-Bass.

Lewin, Kurt, Lippit, Ronald and White, R. K.
    1939   "Patterns of Aggressive Behavior in Experimentally Created Social Climates." Source data unavailable.

McGregor, Douglas
    1960   **The Human Side of Enterprise.** New York: McGraw-Hill Book Company.

Mintzberg, Henry
    1983   **Power In and Around Organizations.** Englewood Cliffs, N. J.: Prentice Hall.

Powers, Bruce
    1979   **Christian Leadership.** Nashville: Broadman Press.

Richards, L. O. and Hoeldtke, Clyde
    1980   **A Theology of Church Leadership.** Grand Rapids: Zondervan Publishing House.

Shawchuck, Norman
    1983   "Are You A Flexible Leader?" **Leadership.** Spring 1983.

Toffler, Alvin
    1970   **Future Shock.** New York: Bantam.

Weber, Max
    1957   **The Theory of Social and Economic Organization.** Translated by A. H. Henderson and Talcott Parsons. Glencoe, IL: Free Press.

Wrong, Dennis
    1980   **Power Its Forms, Bases and Uses.** New York: Harper and Row.

Yukl, Gary A.
1981   **Leadership In Organizations**. Englewood Cliffs, NJ: Prentice Hall, Inc.

CPSIA information can be obtained
at www.ICGtesting.com
Printed in the USA
BVOW08s0806220217
476861BV00001B/28/P